The
Magical
MENAGERIE

ABOUT THE AUTHOR

Mike Leslie holds master's degrees in occupational psychology and psychotherapy, and has worked in counseling, psychiatric nursing, and psychotherapy. Currently he is a psychiatric nurse with extensive experience in psychological assessment in both clinical and nonclinical settings. He lives in England.

The
Magical
MENAGERIE

Personal Power Through Animal Energies

Mike Leslie
Illustrations by Eric Hotz

Llewellyn Publications
St. Paul, Minnesota

First Edition
First Printing, 2005

Cover art © 2004 by Eric Hotz
Cover design by Ellen Dahl
Editing by Connie Hill
Interior card illustrations © 2004 by Eric Hotz

Library of Congress Cataloging-in-Publication Data
Leslie, Mike, 1956–
    The magical menagerie : personal power through animal energies / Mike
  Leslie ; illustrations by Eric Hotz
      p.   cm.
  Includes bibliographical references.
  ISBN 0-7387-0505-5
    1. Magic. 2. Animals—Miscellanea.   3. Animals, Mythical—Miscellanea.
  I. Title.

BF1623.A55L47   2005
133.4'3—DC22   2004057746

Llewellyn Publications
A Division of Llewellyn Worldwide, Ltd.
P.O. Box 64383, Dept. 0-7387-0505-5
St. Paul, MN 55164-0383, U.S.A.
www.llewellyn.com

Printed in the United States of America

CONTENTS

Introduction

A bestiary is a treatise on real and mythological animals. Bestiaries became popular in the Middle Ages and were the most frequently produced books after the bible and other religious texts. They seem to have originated in second-century Alexandria with the *Physiologus*, a collection of forty-eight stories about animals.

The *Magical Menagerie* is concerned with creatures of magical significance and includes the familiar ones of this world as well as the fabulous ones of the Otherworld. The bestiary is based on the ancient system of elements, and each of these elements is represented by its respective elemental. Most of the mythological animals described here originated in ancient Greece, although they were well known to medieval wizards.

The other, more familiar animals featured here are drawn from Celtic myth. These animals continued to have special occult significance in medieval Europe long after the ancient Celtic cultures that venerated them had ceased to exist. In European tradition they are known as familiars, and they have a similar function to the power animals of Native American traditions.

Each beast described here epitomizes particular spiritual qualities that may be operative in your life at any given time. As the title suggests, the system is of particular interest to modern wizards who wish to divine prevailing influences before commencing magical work. However, *The Magical Menagerie* may be used by anyone who wants to develop an understanding of current influences on their life, or to ask questions about the future.

In my book *The Magical Personality* (Llewellyn, 2002), I describe magic as essentially a psychological event. The magician's personality is considered to be the pivotal factor in determining the type of magic to which the magician is best adapted, and consequently which aims are most likely to succeed. Personality is described in terms of the four elements of the ancient world: Earth, Air, Fire, and Water (five if Quintessence is included). Two of these four tend to be relatively well developed and conscious, the other two relatively undeveloped and unconscious.

The developed, conscious pairs are described with reference to mythical beasts that illustrate the positive qualities of a given type. The undeveloped, unconscious pairs are also described with reference to these beasts but as negative shadow types. Thus, any individual may be described in positive and negative terms, using all four elements. The primary type indicates strengths, the shadow type indicates potential weaknesses in both ordinary and magical life.

This model therefore predicts success or failure on the basis of personality development. Other factors such as time and place are regarded as of secondary importance. However, this does not mean that external factors are of no importance. Indeed, the most important external variables are the spiritual agencies that facilitate the work and bring it to conclusion. Which of these is most amenable to the magician's goal and which ones may most easily be contacted is a function of the magician's own personality in line with the principle of empathy. The familiars in the bestiary are also described in terms of the elements of Fire, Water, Earth, and Air, just as the magician may be, with implications for this empathic link.

Other card decks, with one or two exceptions, feature exclusively mundane creatures. *The Magical Menagerie* includes fantastic beasts such as the Unicorn and Mermaid, as well as elemental Gnomes, Undines, Salamanders, and Sylphs. The system therefore puts at the wizard's disposal a means of divining prevalent Otherworld forces—from the elemental and stable to the more sophisticated, but relatively unstable. The qualities of time and place may thus be determined.

ONE

The Magical Menagerie

The Magical Menagerie card deck consists of the elemental Gnomes, Undines, Salamanders and Sylphs. In addition there are cards representing the fifth element Quintessence and a Fetch, or artificial elementary. There are the twelve mythical beasts that first appeared in my book, *The Magical Personality*. Finally there are twenty-four animal spirits derived from the Celtic tradition. This makes forty-two cards in all. They are read either upright or reversed and separate meanings are given accordingly.

THE ANCIENT WORLD VIEW

The Magical Menagerie is based on the system of primary elements: Earth, Air, Fire, and Water. This categorical system originated in ancient Greece and was used to describe the entire universe. On the face of it, the theory of the elements seems hopelessly archaic until equated with modern ideas. All matter exists in solid form (Earth), as liquid (Water), or as gas (Air), and everything is a particular pattern of energy

(Fire). This ancient system was adopted by Western Europe and used right up until modern times when it finally fell into disuse when modern science began to develop. However, this system continues to have value and application in our own time in the context of mythic understanding of the self and the universe.

The medieval worldview envisaged a great "Chain of Being" that stretched up from the lowest forms in each realm of animal, vegetable, and mineral to God himself, an idea that also originated with the Greeks. In Greek legend, Zeus lowered a golden chain down to Homer, thereby establishing a link between the physical world and the gods. Most beings were composed of imperfect mixes of the elements and were thus unstable. This not only conferred particular qualities on them but also meant that they did not live forever, unlike the angelic beings. Human beings were of course included in this scheme and were also considered to be imperfect mixtures of the elements, as temperamental differences and mortality indicated.

THE ELEMENTS AND PSYCHOLOGY

The equivalence of the ancient elements with basic states of being is only one way in which this ancient system can be seen to have a modern application. The idea of psychological temperaments is derived from the theory of the elements, and has its best exponent in the figure of the great Swiss psychologist C. G. Jung, who was a great believer in the validity of ancient wisdom. The ancient Greeks referred to psychological correlates of the elements believed to be rooted in biological substrates called humours. In this system, a choleric (fiery) temperament was believed to be caused by an excess of yellow bile, a sanguine (airy) temperament by too much blood, a phlegmatic (watery) temperament by too much phlegm, and a melancholy (earthy) temperament by too much black bile. Physical and psychological health were assumed to depend on a correct balance of these humours.

One of Jung's many contributions to modern psychology was to consider the temperaments as basic psychological attributes. In Jung's system the psyche is organized in terms of the functions of sensing, thinking, intuition, and feeling. Sensing, as the word suggests, is related to the senses. Information is derived from sense impressions of the physical world in the present. Thinking refers to logical analysis of available facts. Intuition, by contrast, refers to direct insight into patterns and future possibilities. Feeling naturally refers to the notion of personal values in perception and decision making. Jung's system has been widely used in psychotherapy, counseling, education, and industry. It is not difficult to see how these psychological functions may be associated with the ancient elements.

THE ELEMENTS AND ASTROLOGY

Jung (1966) famously stated that astrology is the sum total of all the psychological wisdom of the ancients. Astrology had long ago incorporated the elements to provide a rich system with which to understand the self and one's place in the cosmic scheme. Writers such as Arroyo (*Astrology, Psychology, and the Four Elements*, CRCS Publications, 1975) have contributed greatly to our understanding of the elements as building blocks of astrological thought and application in the modern world.

The elements are basic to astrology, a system that offers a way of understanding the self and the universe in mythic terms. The elements have three modalities called triplicities and twelve primary patterns called signs. The triplicities refer to action in time; fixed signs are concerned with the present, mutable signs are concerned with shifting energy that moves back to connect with the past or forward to connect with the future, and cardinal signs refer to future-directed action. The modalities and the patterns combine to offer a rich and varied expression of human experience. Each individual sign is characterized by a particular attunement that Arroyo equates with archetypal forces. I strongly recommend Arroyo's book to anyone interested in the elemental basis of astrology.

THE ELEMENTS IN EVERYDAY LIFE

The elements can be seen to map onto basic areas of our lives. Earth represents the material world, our physical health, work, finances, home, and even the types of food we eat. Air represents our minds, our reason, analytical qualities, education, and the realm of ideas and creativity, the conscious mind. Water represents our emotions, artistic sensitivity, aesthetic concerns, dreams, and the unconscious mind. Fire represents our energy, drive, motivation, and sheer zest for life. More importantly as the New Age gathers pace the elements can be seen to represent spiritual qualities that can be called upon to guide us. Figure 1 summarizes these ideas graphically.

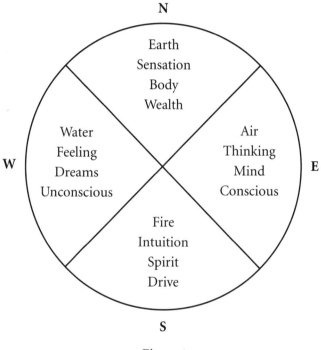

Figure 1

The Magical Personality describes how the elements can be described as psychological characteristics or temperaments. *The Magical Menagerie* describes how they can indicate qualities of time and space, as well as the nature of spiritual entities. The elements are considered to possess the following qualities:

> Earth is cold and dry
> Water is cold and moist
> Air is hot and moist
> Fire is hot and dry

As well as these qualities, the elements vary according to their levels of energy and duration. Thus, Earth is both lowest in energy and most durable, Fire most energetic and least durable. It is on this basis that the attributes of time and place may be divined.

COMBINATIONS OF ELEMENTS

The effect of interactions among the elements is important, and the following offers some pointers concerning benefits and tensions that may arise.

Earth with Earth produces a highly stable, solid, and conventional combination that may be prone to materialism and inertia.

Earth with Water can be a fertile combination. The expansive nature of Water is contained by the practical Earth, which benefits from the gift of compassion. Tension arises from the dreaminess of Water and the pragmatism of Earth.

Earth with Air benefits from the blending of pragmatism with inventiveness, but only if the ideas generated are realistic.

Earth with Fire leads to stimulation of the sluggish Earth and limiting of the expansive nature of Fire. Great productiveness results as long as the cold, slow Earth does not fall out with the hot, quick Fire.

Water with Water produces a beautiful, loving, understanding relationship that can suffer from oversensitivity and an inability to deal with mundane realities.

Water with Air leads to a wonderful combination of reason and compassion, ideas and creativity. This is as long as the balance is good, otherwise one faculty may overpower the other.

Water with Fire seems unlikely in combination, but we are considering qualities, not actual Fire and Water. Both are expansive, so this is enhanced. Both are visionary. Once again the balance is delicate, the passion of Fire possibly at variance with the sensitivity of Water.

Air with Air is characterized by a love of learning, intellectual pursuits, and analysis, but tending ultimately to shallowness and impermanence.

Air with Fire is a productive combination in which ideas receive the impetus of Fire. The danger lies in the loss of control that may result in overexcitement and burnout.

Fire with Fire naturally produces a combination characterized by great energy, a heady flow of inspiration, and passion that can be intense but short-lived.

TWO LINKED TRADITIONS

The Magical Menagerie therefore reflects the Greek legacy combined with Celtic lore. Although the theory of elements is derived from ancient Greece, it is evident that the ancient Celts venerated the elemental forces of nature. The Greeks typically took an intellectual approach while the Celts retained an essentially mystical outlook. The Celtic veneration of Water, particularly sacred pools, is well known, as are the Fire festivals such as Beltane and Samhain. Earth and sky forces were also venerated in the form of great dragons, as was the case in ancient China.

It appears that the Celts and the Greeks were familiar with each other's culture. There are even ancient Greek records that state that Greek philosophy, including that of Pythagoras, was heavily influenced by that of the Druids (Berresford, Ellis, P., *A Brief History of the Celts,* 2003). Hippolytus seems to have held the philosophical teachings of the Druids in high regard. A possible Greek influence has also been noted in the design of the monoliths at Stonehenge.

THE ARTHURIAN CONNECTION

The animals described here are among the most prominent of those venerated by the Celts, and are the ones that have remained important in folk magic throughout Europe. Although the druids had been destroyed and their teachings lost, the mystical ideas associated with common plants and animals survived in folklore and also found their way into literature. Many of the animals in the menagerie are prominent in *The Mabinogian* and the various works concerning King Arthur, such as Mallory's *Le Morte D'Arthur.*

Of particular interest in this regard is the earliest of the Arthurian tales that is found in the *Mabinogian,* "Culhwch and Olwen," in which the lost child Mabon is discovered with the help of sacred animals. First the ancient wisdom of the Blackbird is sought, and he directs Arthur's men to the Stag, who directs them to the Owl, who directs them to the Eagle, who finally directs them to the oldest animal of all, the Salmon. This venerable creature is able to reveal the child's whereabouts.

Other Arthurian tales feature animals as prominent spiritual forces. The White Hart appears in various tales. In one, Arthur rides his horse to death in pursuit of a hart; in another, a hart is accompanied by four lions as it roams through the forest of King Galafres. At the wedding feast of Arthur and Guinevere a white hart appears, pursued by a white hound and a pack of black hounds. Merlin sternly warns Arthur that he must attend to this chase if he is to avoid dishonor.

The English famously do not eat horse flesh, although other Europeans, especially the French, have no qualms about doing so. In the British Isles, at the time of the Celts, the horse was sacred and therefore eating this animal was taboo. The horse was a symbol of the goddess of the land; England has many examples of horses carved into the side of chalk hills. The Irish cult of the horse whisperer is legendary. Naturally the horse is the chief means of pursuing the hart.

Ravens appear in Arthurian tales, principally as harbingers of death through their connection with the Morrighan. Owain has an army of ravens to defend him. The Welsh god Bran's name means raven. According to legend Bran's head was buried at the site of the Tower of London. The Tower's ravens are a favorite tourist attraction, and it is said that should they ever leave, the realm will be destroyed. Arthur himself was alleged to have turned into a raven following his death at Camlan. It is clear from these examples that the mystical importance of the Celtic animals has survived to the present day to exert an effect on popular consciousness.

THE DEVELOPMENT OF
THE MAGICAL MENAGERIE

The origins and development of *The Magical Menagerie* are associated with my attempts to find answers to some pressing questions surrounding my own occult practices. I found in writing *The Magical Personality* that I also needed to balance the perspective of that book with one that stressed the importance of spiritual entities. There were questions such as "What are the prevalent qualities of time and place that may affect a chosen outcome?" "How transient are they?" "Are they likely to help or hinder?" The personality of the magician is important, but it is always interacting with something in order to bring about a desired effect. These other personalities are the focus of this system.

Existing oracles in which spirit animals are portrayed as guides were of some help. However, in dreams, on journeys, and in the call of spirit that often gives rise to unexpected imagery during daydreams, I met not only the familiar creatures of this world but also mythical ones such as Unicorns and Centaurs that exist only in the Otherworld. These seemed to signify something of particular importance beyond the affairs of this world. They were wholly otherworldly and frequently represented something deep and potent. What could help me to understand the appearance of these beings? None of the existing card sets included them. Accordingly, I began experimenting with the divinatory system that developed into *The Magical Menagerie*.

The elements form the basic framework upon which the system is built. I had two reasons for adopting this framework: in the first place I had already used it in creating *The Magical Personality*, in which personality types are characterized as mythical beings. The new work is thus integrated with the previous one. Secondly, the elements are not static, but interact dynamically with each other. This means that the process of change within time and space could be reflected by the system. The direction of transition due to changes in energy is as follows:

Fire (rising)
Air (rising/sinking)
Water (sinking/rising)
Earth (sinking)

Fire is most energetic, but its duration is relatively short unless it has fuel to keep it going—thus it tends to convert to the slower qualities associated with Air. Air may slow further to transform into the qualities associated with

Water, or it may speed up and revert to Fire. Water can likewise speed up or slow down to become Earth, the slowest and most enduring of the states. The appearance of a particular element or elemental combination thus offers a clue to the stability of a given situation temporally, spatially, or both. It hardly needs repeating here that I am not referring to actual Fire, Air, Water, or Earth, but to energy patterns related to spiritual forces.

Each creature can, by its appearance, indicate salient times or directions of increasing specificity. For example, Gnome refers to the north, winter, and night generally. The mythical beasts Centaur, Wodwose, and Gryphon offer more clarity, while the Earthly animals of the Earth quadrant are even more specific, but at the expense of stability. Generally speaking, the more elements involved, the greater the scope for change with secondary, tertiary, and final elements, each exerting a degree of *pull* on the primary element and on each other. The example spreads should make this clearer.

Each creature is placed according to its attributes. This can seem a little confusing at times until the qualities associated with that creature are known. Thus, all the creatures found in the Air quadrant have the same essential primary association with knowledge and wisdom. The apparently odd placing of Salmon among the Air creatures rather than the Water animals is explicable with reference to Celtic myth. The Celts regarded Salmon as the oldest and wisest of all the animals. This fish swam in the pool of Segais and fed on the hazelnuts that fell from the tree of wisdom itself.

All the animals in the Air quadrant are likewise associated with wisdom, albeit in slightly different ways. Wren was revered by the Druids despite being the smallest native bird of the British Isles. It was seen as both resourceful and tenacious, a low-flying, highly territorial bird. This characteristic is reflected by the Earth secondary, while its shyness and tendency to stay low is reflected by Water and Fire in that order. Eagle, on the other hand, is a bird that flies high and is thus associated with vision and foresight. The Fire secondary reflects the reputation of this bird as a fierce predator. With the Earth left far below, it is the least grounded of the Air creatures and Earth is correspondingly less in evidence. Similar descriptions could be made for each of the forty-two creatures that comprise the deck.

I should say a word here about the inclusion of Quintessence and Fetch as part of the system. There are occasionally times when circumstances are exactly right and other times when they go inexplicably wrong. Quintessence reflects the former while Fetch indicates those chaotic, uncertain influences that often have to be endured until they pass away. Usually another reading is required to discover the cause and duration of this uncertainty. The section on spreads includes remedies for such disturbances of place.

TWO

Uses of the Magical Menagerie

The Magical Menagerie can be used for a number of purposes. Like other card decks depicting animal spirits, the pack can be used to identify current important forces in your life or to gain self-understanding. You can use it to clarify problems or as a form of divination. Finally you can use it to help in your magic work.

There are times when we are confused or at a loss over something. At these times it helps to have the wisdom of another person or a guide who can help. In former times it was easier to approach a shaman or wise elder who had the power to commune with the spirits to discover what might be done. The skill of augury and reading omens was possible for anyone who was sufficiently intuitive and sensitive. Now it is less easy because we are so far from the natural world and constantly distracted by the demands of modern life.

It is still possible to use these methods but, as always, it takes practice. Sometimes things happen out of context or coincidentally in such a way as to appear meaningful. Jung mentioned something of this sort in *Memories, Dreams, Reflections* (Fontana, 1983). He relates that he was preoccupied with a picture of a kingfisher that was associated with his guide Philemon. While out walking he found a recently dead kingfisher—near Zurich, where kingfishers are extremely rare.

Despite living in the heart of a city, it is still possible to experience a strange, meaningful occurrence of this sort, most often in dreams, but also in other ways. One way of deliberately encouraging such an occurrence is to use an oracle. You may not see an eagle in town but you may see a symbol of one, or you may draw Eagle from the deck. Guides make themselves known by various means when their help is needed.

Some of the spreads described later do not relate to problems but to matters of personal insight. The maxim "know thyself" is not just sound advice; it is essential. An oracle can be usefully employed in self-discovery and *The Magical Menagerie* is particularly helpful in this regard because all the beasts mentioned are associated with psychological characteristics and personal qualities by virtue of being based on the elements. If you know your own elemental makeup, you can then assess how a particular familiar in a given position speaks to you.

You can get to know different familiars and invite them into your life by meditating on them. By deliberately focusing on the qualities of a particular beast, you will go some way to developing those qualities in yourself as well as welcoming that familiar by the power of attunement. It is also helpful to carry something associated with the creature in question, or to have a picture of it in your home.

While all of the methods described here are forms of divination, the term is usually employed to mean foretelling the future. The authors of most systems state categorically that theirs are not designed to do this, and then go on to describe spreads with final outcome positions that imply that they do indeed foretell the future. There is a good reason for this cautious attitude, apart from the obvious one that the future cannot be predicted. The reason is that predicting the future is an imprecise art. On the other hand we all predict the future most of the time, if only on a statistical basis.

We can successfully predict that we will be somewhere in particular, doing something specific, as long as the predicted event is not too distant. If you usually work on Mondays and say that you will be at work on Monday morning, then you probably will be, but not necessarily. The likelihood of being killed if you fall out of an aircraft at a high altitude is quite high, yet there are numerous accounts of people surviving such falls unharmed, against all the odds.

The future is fluid, unlike the past, which is fixed. The future gels in the present moment before setting hard as the past. Thus, you can divine the future as long as you bear these things in mind—the greater the temporal distance of the event in question, the less easy it is to predict; also, nothing is absolutely certain. The single greatest aid in all divination work is a meditative attitude that will encourage correct perceptions. Always take a little time in which to withdraw from this world so that you can tap into the Otherworld more effectively. The art of divination is considered more fully in the chapter under that heading.

The spreads described here include some that are designed to help identify potentially helpful or unhelpful factors. These may refer to prevalent forces in either world, to time, or to location. Once these factors have been identified, you are in a position to alter matters appropriately. This may mean spiritual cleansing, changing the timing or the location of the work. In this sense the *Menagerie* is like an occult torch that can reveal both helpful and obstructive influences. This is one of the things that makes *The Magical Menagerie* unique.

SPREADS

The simplest spread involves drawing a single card to answer a given query. While this has the advantage of speed, it naturally offers less information than more involved procedures, but it can be very useful, especially when you are getting used to the cards. Single-card spreads are probably the best ones to start with.

A single card can give a quick overview of a situation or give quick answers to questions relating to direction or timing. For example,

Q: What is this person's intention?
A: Fox

The suggestion is that this person is cunning and intelligent but not necessarily. He or she is probably acting on the basis of a primal urge to survive in the most effective way they know.

Q: Is this a good time to cast this spell?
A: Chimera reversed

This suggests that the time does not favor immediate action because of imbalance leading to lack of control and the increased chance of a chaotic outcome. The most auspicious time to work is given by the card, in this case 4 PM.

Another consideration on this point is the recurrence of particular cards in different readings. This naturally suggests that a particular spirit is especially significant at the moment, and may even be a personal familiar. In my own experiments while devising this set, I found Firebird appearing with great frequency. Firebird combines the imaginative qualities of Air with the enthusiasm of Fire. Firebird is creative and wants to produce something that can be useful to others. The system seemed to be confirming itself!

THE THREE-CARD SPREAD

A particularly useful spread uses three cards. This layout fits well with our perception of the passage of time from past, through present, to future. Even when this progression is not a feature of the reading, the three-card spread offers a narrative that is not overly complicated. This spread also gives an indication of the outcome of a question according to whether the cards are upright or reversed. If all three are upright, the answer is positive. If they are all reversed, the answer is negative. If one is reversed, the answer is probably positive, depending on the position of the one reversed card. If there is only one upright card, the answer is probably negative, depending on the position of this card. Obviously the third and final position describes the nature of the outcome.

The three-card spread naturally gives more information. Note first whether the cards are upright or reversed. Three upright cards indicates a definite yes, three reversed a definite no, at least for the time being. Mixed readings suggest that matters are in a state of flux. The position of upright or reversed cards in the spread indicates the direction of positive or negative change. Two reversed cards followed by an upright means that changes are moving toward a positive outcome. Two uprights followed by a final reversed card suggests the opposite. The middle card gives advice on current action as well as describing prevailing conditions. Finally the stability of current conditions is indicated by the nature of the creature that appears, depending on its elemental makeup. Animals of this world suggest greater instability and short-lived states in comparison with the elementals such as Salamander, but take note of which element is predominant—Fire is always less durable than Earth.

EXAMPLE 1:

Q: Should I cast this money spell, and when would
    be the best time?

A: Undine   Dragon   Gnome

Undine in the first position suggests connection with
the deep unconscious and hence with the magical forces.
This is a good first-position card because it shows that the
preparatory work has been done—you are in tune with the
other world forces.

Dragon in second position indicates that the power and
the enthusiasm to bring about change is potent right now
in the present. May 1 at 10 AM would be the optimum time
for the spell, according to this creature.

Gnome in final position is particularly auspicious because the magical goal relates to wealth, but in any case it
suggests that the outcome will be successful because this
card concerns manifestation on the physical plane. Note
also that all three cards are upright, indicating a definite
positive outcome.

Q: Should I contact my friend following our
    argument?

A: Mermaid (R)   Owl   Pegasus

The first card sets the scene in this example. It describes
a situation in which emotional upset and misunderstanding have led to the current impasse. Notice that emotional
Water prevails over rational Air.

The second card suggests a time of transition because it is a four-element creature and the conditions it describes may not last long. It's necessary to take advantage of them while they last. Owl is an Air creature with Water in last place and refers to a state in which thought prevails over emotion. Communication is highlighted as a course of action now that tempers have cooled.

The final card is upright and the elements suggest greater stability characterized by perceptiveness and coming down to Earth. The sequence reads "emotional upset and being unreasonable (Mermaid R), private reconsideration and subsequent communication (Owl), followed by restoration of order, fairness, and openness (Pegasus)." The reading thus advises what best to do and predicts the likely outcome.

Consider the following examples: Anthony was thinking of changing his job. He was working in the accounts division of a local hospital but he had recently qualified as a counselor. Consulting *The Magical Menagerie,* he drew:

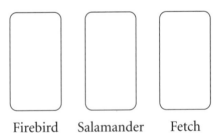

Firebird   Salamander   Fetch

Firebird refers to his desire to change jobs in order to do something more meaningful to him. It's an Air card combined with Fire indicating ideals and passion. This is a card of reform. Salamander is pure Fire, pure urgency and drive. Anthony was itching to get on and do it. Fetch however indicated that the future was uncertain with respect to this question. The advice therefore was for Anthony to curb his enthusiasm and exercise some caution. Unexpected financial worries suddenly caused him to put his job change on hold.

A further spread yielded:

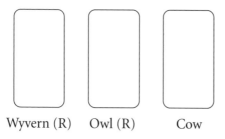

Wyvern (R)   Owl (R)   Cow

The two reversed cards suggest that current conditions are unfavorable. Wyvern refers to injustice among other things, and Anthony did indeed feel that the financial burden was unfair. Owl suggested that the immediate outlook was not good. However, Cow in the final position suggested money. Eventually the new financial year brought funding for a new counselor post so Anthony didn't even have to move when he finally took up the new job.

THE FOUR-CARD SPREAD

A four-card layout is useful for questions concerning matters of guidance, as well as for questions concerning locations. Lay out four cards as shown with Earth/north at the top (it's easier if you face north for this), and place the other cards in the Air/east, Fire/south, Water/west positions.

Lynda was curious to see what the cards would say about her elemental makeup and the implications for her day-to-day life. She drew the following:

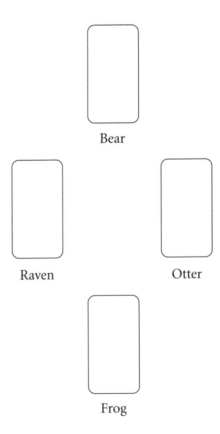

Bear

Raven   Otter

Frog

The first thing to note is that there are three Water cards, suggesting that Lynda is an emotional person who probably makes her feelings the basis of her decision making. Bear is an Earth card and it appears in the Earth quadrant. The suggestion is that Lynda is a practical, down-to-earth sort of person who is not easily sidetracked from her goals. More precisely Bear refers to protection. Lynda found this easy to relate to because she is a mother of two small children, but she is also fiercely protective of her friends.

Otter is a Water card in the Air quadrant. Otter refers to fun and enjoyment, while Air is more concerned with sober rationalism and learning. Lynda agreed that she had never been attracted to study because she was too busy having fun to get bogged down with dry academic matters. She is also led by her heart rather than her head, as protective Bear confirmed.

Frog is a Water card in the Fire quadrant. Frog refers to sensitivity while Fire refers to energy and drive. Both are expansive elements, but Frog indicates caution and some emotional rawness. Lynda is not, therefore, one to rush ahead and always considers how she and others will be affected by her actions. Finally Raven is a Water card in the Water quadrant, which reinforces the Water theme in Lynda's personality.

Raven is a card of prophecy and connection with the Otherworld. Lynda said that she had had some strange experiences and she often believed she was psychic. Her feeling nature is in keeping with this idea and it may be that she has a special gift to develop.

The following example illustrates how the cards can be used to assess a location. This may be necessary if there is an uncomfortable atmosphere, it seems to attract bad luck, or if you intend to work magic there. Various cures can then be employed similar to those used in Feng Shui (see below).

When my wife and I moved into a new home, we both immediately felt a presence, especially in the lounge. Other people mentioned feeling this, and one woman even saw a fleeting image of a young woman wearing clothes in the style of the early 1960s. The presence felt benign, but was nonetheless puzzling. I was developing the *Menagerie* at the time and decided to use it to explore the lounge area. The reading was as follows:

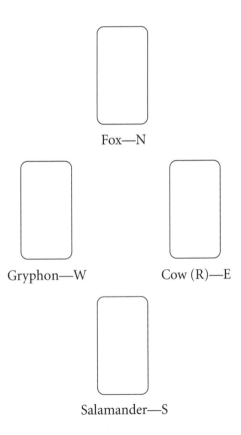

Fox—N

Gryphon—W   Cow (R)—E

Salamander—S

The most important feature of the reading concerned the western area of the room where the presence was felt most strongly and also where the apparition had been seen. Gryphon is an Earth creature and is a fierce protector, especially of property. Interestingly the only reversed card was Cow directly opposite in the eastern sector. Cow is also an Earth card but reversed it represents poverty, loss, and antisocial behavior. It looked as if the protective Gryphon was protecting not only the entrance to the lounge but, more importantly, the weak eastern area. Here the room gave access to the front yard via French doors, and beyond that lay the street.

Fox, also a watchful, protective creature, was located in the north. The south was represented by Salamander, the Fire elemental.

Although a number of homes nearby were burgled, ours never was, despite being an obvious target. Nevertheless we decided to make the place more secure, following which I again diagnosed the room with this result:

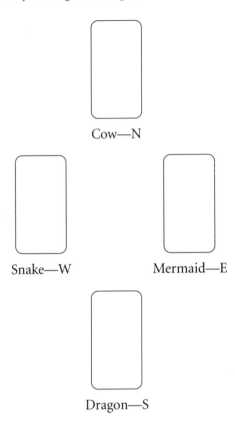

Cow—N

Snake—W   Mermaid—E

Dragon—S

Now Gryphon had been replaced by Snake, another guardian animal, but one associated with regeneration. The east was now occupied by Mermaid, a creature concerned with the welfare of others and in direct contrast with the previous Cow (R). Cow, meanwhile, appeared upright in the north. An Earth creature associated with wealth settled in the Earth area, suggesting that the property was now secure. With Dragon, a Fire animal in the fiery south, the room was more balanced.

The net result is that we retained our guardian in a different form, but the room was more mellow and relaxing. Note that we changed the tone of the room with purely practical measures in the problem area.

A five-card spread is most useful for guidance issues. The cards are arranged in the form of a pentagram and related to the elements (including Quintessence). A particular use for the five-card spread is the discovery of personal familiars. It is part of established lore in magic that wizards and shamen have spirit helpers, usually in the form of an animal. The best way to identify your familiar is to go on an Otherworld journey. You may also find that a particular animal appears frequently in dreams or coincidentally during everyday activities.

The cards can be used in similar fashion since the system is predicated on the basis that particular animals are trying to make themselves known to you as guides and helpers. The elements refer to areas of life where you may find you are being helped or where you need help, and the apex card reveals your familiar, or power animal. If you already know your familiar, place that card in the apex position and deal a card to each element to discover your other helpers and guides. These tend to change according to circumstances, while the personal familiar remains with us for many years, or even for life.

Ruby drew the following cards:

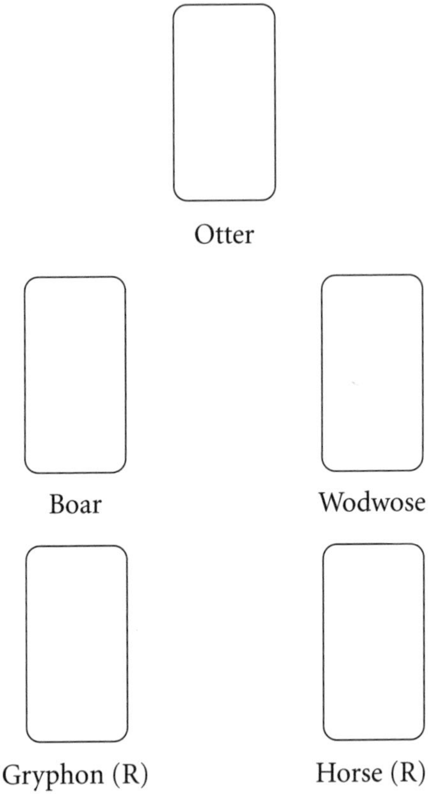

Otter

Boar

Wodwose

Gryphon (R)

Horse (R)

1. Quintessence or apex card. Otter represents playfulness and pleasure. Ruby was surprised to get this card because she doesn't have much time for play in her work-orientated life. The obvious explanation is that Otter has appeared in such a prominent position because she needs to relax and enjoy social activities rather than just working all the time.

2. Earth. Here we find Horse reversed, an Earth card in the Earth sphere. This card ties in with the one above to underscore the sense of overwork. In the area of material concerns, Ruby has been wearing herself out.

3. Air. Boar is a Fire card in the Air position. Boar refers to strength, combat, fearlessness, and tenacity. In the sphere of the intellect, it indicates someone who knows her own mind and isn't afraid to speak up in defense of self or others. Her logic is impeccable and her power in this area is formidable. Ruby is not the kind of person you would want to argue with!

4. Fire. Wodwose is an Earth card in the Fire position. Once again the theme of work and productiveness is found. All Ruby's energy goes into bringing forth tangible results. This is not in itself a bad thing but the overall message of the reading is that Ruby needs to balance work and play.

5. Water. Gryphon is an Earth card in the Water position. Gryphon reversed refers to fear of financial instability and the lack of security that this entails. The

fact that it is in the emotional sphere indicates the motive force behind the idea. Ruby recognized the implication—in attempting to maintain her material security at the expense of a proper social life she risked undermining her health so that she could not work.

It is notable how the spirits represented by the cards can serve to warn of such a state of affairs. The reversed cards are in this sense friendly because they act like counselors, encouraging us to pay attention to imbalance and personal need.

TIME

Change occurs over time, the reason time factors are often more important than those relating to place. The qualities of a place may, in fact, alter according to the passage of time, a fact that may be readily observed from spending a day in the same room. You will notice that the atmosphere changes as the pattern of light and temperature shifts from morning to afternoon to night. Changes within ourselves occur on a temporal basis and are known as circadian rhythms. Our changing selves are in a constant relationship to our changing environment at all times.

Timing is crucial when planning any event. The well-worn adage that timing is the secret of comedy is a case in point. There is plenty of well-established magical lore relating to time factors, one of the most important being the phases of the moon, but including planetary hours throughout the day and night. These are general guides and do not offer specific information regarding your personal circumstances. The *Menagerie* is designed to shed light on these more personal factors.

Each animal in the deck is associated not only with a direction, but also a time period. In the case of the elementals, this is quite vague, referring to "winter," "night," and so on. The mythical beasts are a little more specific and the Earthly animals are relatively precise. Time factors, as they relate to your personal circumstances, can thus be divined quickly and easily using one of the spreads below. This can be quite helpful if you need to cast spells urgently but are unsure of prevailing temporal tides, or your intuition may be warning you against something even though the moon phase and the planetary hour, etc., are auspicious.

As always, a single card gives an instant answer to questions such as "What is the best time to work this magic?" or "Is this a good time to cast this spell." The time indicated by the card selected gives the answer. As ever, take note of whether the card is upright or reversed. Reversed cards generally indicate unfavorable times.

The three-card spread can be used in exactly the same way as for place (see example given earlier). More emphasis is placed on the flow from past through present to future. Take special note of the elemental makeup of the beasts as they appear.

Another way of inquiring into time conditions is to ask about events that may occur in the future. Each position then relates to a particular time frame, whether it's a year, a month, a week, a day, or an hour. Spreads of appropriate lengths can be employed accordingly. For example, a commonly used spread covers the months of the year as shown below.

Lay out the cards in a circle beginning with the upcoming month; if you are reading in December, the first month is January. If you read on Halloween, the first month is November, and so on. When laying the cards in a circle, have upright cards with heads pointing toward the center and reversed cards with heads pointing away from the center. Place a final card in the middle to represent an overall influence for the year to come.

Twelve- (or twenty-four-) card spreads can be used to assess the hours of the day or night. A seven-card spread will likewise represent the week ahead and a four-card spread will cover the weeks of the month or the seasonal quarters. In this way you will not only have an insight into what is to come for each time period, but you can see which period is most likely to fit with your magical activities.

CURES

Having identified potential problem areas, it becomes possible to tackle them. The deliberate attempt at contacting relevant familiars by meditation and other empathic methods is the most direct. Physical spaces can be treated the same way by communing in the specific location(s), or by performing cleansing operations using incense, candles, bells, or whatever seems appropriate. You can even use the cards themselves to promote particular ties. By having a specific card in, say, the northern part of the room, every time you see it the familiar and its qualities will be brought to mind.

THREE

The Art of Divination

Divination is a procedure for clarifying the obscure by means of oracles and augury. The word is derived from "divine," which refers to something that relates to or is provided by a god or goddess. Undertaken in the right spirit, divination is therefore a holy act. If we follow the teachings of the mystics or the ideas of theoretical physicists, we can accept that we are not only part of the universe but that we each encapsulate the universe. The ancients proposed that the microcosm contains the macrocosm in miniature. The idea of the holographic universe proposes that each particle contains the whole. This being so, each of us already knows the answer to any given question because it lies within us. The problem lies in seeing the answer with sufficient clarity to make practical use of it. In connection with this, I am reminded of the Chandogya Upanishad 8.1, in which we are extolled to find who dwells in the center of our heart. The writer says that in our heart is a castle, and in the castle is a shrine. In the shrine is a lotus flower, and the center of this flower is as vast as the universe. The stars are there, and all the planets and the sun and the moon, because everything is in Brahma, and he dwells in our heart.

Some analogies may be helpful here. In psychotherapy the unconscious is regarded as the hidden region of the mind that *knows* what it is that ails the patient and how the problem may be ameliorated. It is the purpose of therapy to make conscious that which is unconscious, and this involves the skills of a third party in the person of the therapist. Some therapists make use of the Rorschasch ink blot test as a tool. The idea behind this is that although the conscious mind sees only ink blots, the unconscious mind *sees* an image of the underlying conflict. The therapist then draws these images to the attention of the patient.

The seer frequently uses tools such as cards in order to bypass the real-world focus of the conscious mind and tap into the knowledge of the universal mind. It's rather like trying to see a star in the night sky. If you look directly at it, the fovea or blind spot that is so useful for daytime vision obscures the star, so you have to look to one side of it rather than directly at it. Divination is therefore a means of indirectly revealing what is hidden.

Although many people reveal themselves to be superstitious, whether knowingly or not, we inheritors of the Western tradition of enlightened rationalism tend on the whole to scoff at anything that doesn't agree with the orderly, cause-and-effect universe that is described by Newtonian physics. Magic and divination naturally fall into the category of superstitious nonsense. Scientific thinking throughout the twentieth century, however, led further away from the clock-work universe as popularly accepted and closer to a mystical conception that in some respects resembles the irrational perspective that prevailed prior to the Enlightenment.

There is good reason for this. The rationalist model of the universe is incomplete and does not account for some of the phenomena now known to modern science. The great advantage of the modernist endeavor was that it al-lowed a greater understanding of some aspects of the uni-verse, and this understanding paid off in terms of scientific and technological advances that we now take for granted. What the postmodern view articulates is that there is no right answer or final understanding toward which we can advance. There is not one, but an infinity of explanations, of realities.

The twentieth century began with Einstein's theories about time being relative and space being *bent,* continued with quantum mechanics and the Heisenberg principle, and ended with chaos theory and the realization that order and disorder are inextricably linked. With chaos theory we finally arrived at a science of the random—a contradiction in terms for the classical physicists.

Divination involves revealing that which is apparently random or hidden—the occult. Where conscious thought relates to the *ordinary* world of cause and effect and the fast-flowing river of linear time, the unconscious relates to the extraordinary, to synchronicity, and to what the Chi-nese referred to as "timeless time." Divination makes exten-sive use of symbols and random allocation to sidestep the conscious mind in order to access this lake of boundless time. Symbols are glyphs of aspects of the universe, the archetypes that mirror the state of the universe.

Following recent developments in theoretical physics, it's beginning to look as though the enlightened rationalism of which the West is so proud is something of an aberration. In fact the rationalist, modernist position may seem absurd to the generations of the future, much as the thinking of the *primitive* earlier generations appeared fanciful and naïve to our enlightened forefathers. The rationalism that came to dominate Western thinking only achieved prominence in the eighteenth century and lasted only two centuries before coming up against the challenges of the twentieth century. Those ancient *irrationalists*, the shaman and the mystic, are now being joined by postmodernist thinkers in the twenty-first century.

FOUR

The Menagerie

The magical creatures illustrated and discussed here epitomize spiritual energies and currents that may be an influence in your life at a specific time. The menagerie is a resource that may be used to develop a familiarity with animal energies as they affect an individual or situation, and as an aid to divining the future.

The illustrations here combine simplicity of expression with potency, in themselves a magical event. I had enjoyed working with illustrator Eric Hotz on my previous book *The Magical Personality,* and was very pleased to have him accept the assignment to create the images for this deck.

QUINTESSENCE

Upright: Harmony, balance

This card has no reversed meaning

Direction: the center

Time: eternity

Pace of Change: indicates either that a state of balance
has been attained, or that this state will be reached
suddenly in the very near future

QUINTESSENCE · HARMONY

Quintessence means "fifth element," and refers to the ether or spiritual substrate from which the four elements and indeed all things arise. No beast as such represents Quintessence and it is more appropriate to associate it with the mysterious, imperceptible, awe-inspiring power of pure spirit. As such it represents perfect balance and the direct apperception of the ultimate truth behind appearances. This is the mystical union in which all division is seen as illusory, all striving becomes unnecessary. This is a highly significant omen. It may indicate a need to stop and contemplate the inner truth, to look beyond the manifest world to something higher. Significant changes may be coming that will alter everything for the good.

GNOME
Earth

Upright: the physical, pleasure of the senses, the natural world, riches

Reversed: materialism, skepticism, overindulgence, physical neglect

Direction: north

Time: winter, midnight

Pace of Change: very slow

GNOME · SENSING

Gnomes are the spirits of the Earth element. They are humanoid and appear much as folklore depicts them, as small people who live underground. In Ireland they are known as leprechauns. Earth is the element with which we are most familiar because we are ourselves physical beings that are dependent on the physical world for our continued existence. If we do not eat properly we suffer from malnutrition and eventually death from starvation.

Gnome indicates manifestation on the physical plane and attention to the environment. They represent the things of the earth—riches, wealth, and security. More importantly Gnome indicates that earthly delights may be a path to the spiritual. Thus, it is possible to work, build, amass wealth, and enjoy the fruits of our labors, as long as we do not become slaves to these things or fall into the trap of believing that there is nothing beyond what we can possess. We are ourselves temporarily incarnated as part of the manifest world, and although as physical beings we can enjoy the sensuous and material, it is clear that we must eventually leave it all behind and reenter the hollow hills.

The appearance of Gnome may therefore be an indication that you should enjoy the physical world more. Gnome is your guide. Connect with the spirit of the earth by carrying a piece of metal or a stone—it doesn't have to be of the precious variety. Even a piece of wood with a simple glyph carved on it will help. Go out and acquaint yourself with the natural world. Meditate on the earth and its qualities.

The appearance of Gnome reversed may indicate that there is an overreliance on the physical as a source of satisfaction and self-definition. You are what you eat, but you are not what you own. You are not even your physical body, although earthy types tend to think that they are that and nothing more. There may therefore be overindulgence and materialism at the expense of spiritual concerns. Gnome reversed also suggests poverty and insecurity. Reversed Gnome reflects a grasping, miserly, and selfish attitude. It can also indicate someone who is dour, cold, aloof, and lacking in humor. It can also suggest depression or physical illness and the incapacity that attends these ailments.

UNDINE
Water

Upright: feelings, emotions, connection,
the unconscious, dreams

Reversed: coldness, insensitivity, loneliness, tension

Direction: west

Time: fall, sunset

Pace of Change: quick to start with, slowing suddenly

UNDINE · FEELING

Undines are the spirits of the Water element. They typically take the form of mermaids but may appear simply as liquid swirls. Humans naturally feel close to the water element because our composition is 80 percent water. We can only live for a matter of days without drinking. The other reason for feeling an affinity with water is that we are born with a set of emotions that come and go like the tides of the sea.

Undine therefore refers to emotions, feelings, and interpersonal relations. Undine indicates close relationships, love, selfless devotion, and social harmony. Undine relates to personal empathy, sensitivity, and emotional support. This elemental also indicates artistic inspiration and expression, as well as the psychic arts and mysticism. Undine is inquisitive and possessed of a deep longing to go beyond the confines of current experience. Undine indicates that the deep unconscious is accessible and its images ready to be deciphered.

The appearance of Undine may show a strong urge to connect, either with other people on an emotional level or with the realms of the unconscious and the unseen. Undine will help you. Carry something symbolic of the Water element. There are some attractive glass pendants available, and few people realize that glass is a liquid. Spend time swimming or meditating close to water in order to become more familiar with the characteristics of this element and its messengers.

Undine reversed can indicate emotional coldness, insensitivity, and lack of warmth. Perhaps you feel isolated and in need of companionship. There is a danger of a lack of understanding between people and thus a lack of connection. Sometimes in close relationships love turns to hate, so beware of this change if you have recently felt rejected or hurt. Artistic expression may be affected and inspiration blocked. The occult realms seem cut off and there is a danger either of not having access to the Otherworld or of being so deep within it that life in this world is ignored. Signs and portents from the Otherworld may be confusing or frightening. Relax and reconnect.

SYLPH
Air

Upright: thought, logic, analysis, learning, the conscious

Reversed: false logic, ignorance, narrowness, pedantry

Direction: east

Time: spring, sunrise

Pace of Change: slow at first, becoming rapid

SYLPH · THINKING

Sylphs are the spirits of the Air element. They vary in appearance, sometimes taking the form of butterflies or other insects, sometimes detected as flashes of colored light or simply as tiny swirls in the air. They are usually depicted as female in form. Air is more immediately necessary than water, since we would die within minutes without it. Air represents the intellectual function that exists in us as a potential but which must be cultivated and honed over time.

Sylph refers to thought and to the power of the mind. Knowledge is not by itself sufficient to confer wisdom; understanding is essential, and this suggests insight. However, Sylph does indicate academic matters and understanding acquired through rational analysis and discrimination. Sylph also refers to humanitarian interests, to equality and to civilization. Ultimately, however, Sylphs refers to an understanding of the higher reality behind the illusion of form.

Sylph shows a need to employ the rational power of the thinking faculties. There is information to acquire and make sense of. You may need to consider the evidence in order to discover the truth. Sylph helps with learning and understanding. Carry something that represents the Air element—scent would be ideal. Meditate on the Air element and come to know its qualities.

Sylph reversed indicates stupidity, ignorance, and failure of the intellect. Worse still, it can point toward inability to go beyond observable facts to appreciate the higher truth. Concrete thinking predominates at the expense of abstraction. Wisdom is sacrificed to intellectual arrogance. There is no compassion for the rest of humanity, perhaps not for other life-forms. Everything is reduced to vapid theory. Discrimination can mean prejudice and unreasonable hatred. Lack of discrimination can mean confusion.

SALAMANDER
Fire

Upright: energy, enthusiasm, drive, motivation, speed

Reversed: lack of motivation, lethargy
or hyperactivity, grandiosity

Direction: south

Time: summer, midday

Pace of Change: very fast

SALAMANDER · INTUITION

Salamander is the spirit of the Fire element. Their appearance varies, depending on circumstance, sometimes appearing as firey humanoids, sometimes as black lizards. Fire is even more necessary to us than Air, since without energy we are dead matter, and without the divine spark we are nothing at all. Salamander is naturally representative of energy, heat, power, and passion. Intuition here refers to the psychological characteristic of openness and a tendency to look forward to what is possible.

Salamander indicates a need for passion, drive, speed and intensity. Perhaps you feel restless and are constantly seeking expansion beyond existing limits. This elemental suggests that vitality, vibrancy, social contact, decisive leadership, and direction is called for. Salamander suggests a clear focus and getting things done in the shortest possible time. Salamander is also the power of spirit and the purity of the Divine, so action is in the service of high ideals. The emphasis is on moral and ethical demands.

The appearance of Salamander suggests that energy, passion, and urgency are prominent in your life. Perhaps now is the time to answer the call of the Otherworld. Encourage Salamander to be your guide at this time of furious change. Keep symbols of Fire about your person. Wear Fire-related colors. Dance, be active, and be open to the boundless power of the universe. Meditate on Fire and develop an understanding of this element in your life.

Salamander reversed indicates lack of energy, slowness, coldness, and lack of motivation. Lethargy has taken the place of enthusiasm, and there is little interest in moving beyond known boundaries. The spark of life is dim, and all seems dark and pointless. Sometimes however it may refer to overzealousness and hyperactivity, an unhealthy mania for enjoyment and pleasure-seeking without heeding the costs. There may be loss of faith in the Divine, or alternatively, there may be dangerous ego inflation and spiritual grandiosity.

CENTAUR
Earth and Water

Upright: skill, service, perfection, healing

Reversed: ineptitude, confusion, injury

Direction: north northwest

Time: November, Samhain, 10 PM

Pace of Change: rapid at first, stopping suddenly

CENTAUR · SKILL

The Centaur is half man and half horse and is one of the most familiar of fabulous creatures. In Greek myth, Chiron was a great teacher of many diverse skills. He taught the art of war and the art of healing, music, and divination. Centaur therefore stands for the wisdom of the great teacher.

Centaur represents practical application of skills in the service to others. The primary Earth confers pragmatism and a desire for perfection while Water indicates the area in which skills are employed. Centaur is a teacher, a healer, a warrior, and a seer. All these skills are offered to the community as a service. Centaur is caring but realistic. The skills of the Centaur depend on precise observation, hence caution, analysis, and synthesis, the systematic ordering of information derived from the senses—decisions and actions based on direct experience. Centaur is motivated by a strong sense of duty and is therefore both thorough and dependable. There is a particular urge to nurture the minds of the young. Water also confers a sympathetic and compassionate outlook. Centaur desires to promote cooperation and reciprocation, is sociable but relatively restrained. Allied to this are the gifts of music and a strong sense of aesthetics. When all else fails, Centaur can be relied upon to restore order through the judicious force of arms.

The other side of the Centaur is bestial and rampant. The very blood of the Centaur Nessus was enough to kill Hercules. Centaur reversed means lack of ability or skills used unwisely. The careful approach is replaced by unrealistic, confused, and chaotic methods. Application is careless, insensitive, and haphazard. Centaur reversed is irresponsible and lacks wisdom, has little sense of duty or social obligation, and is self-indulgent. Reversed, Centaur is too cynical, rejecting anything that cannot be registered by the senses. This is the rule of the ignorant and the narrow-minded pedagogue who is without vision. Far from being sympathetic and compassionate, this Centaur sows the seeds of discord. Others are rejected for being different. This is also the sign of the Philistine who has no appreciation of beauty or the arts. Often it warns of contamination and sickness.

WODWOSE
Earth and Fire

Upright: manifestation, gradual development, tenacity

Reversed: inertia, failure, selfishness

Direction: north

Time: December, winter solstice, midnight

Pace of Change: slowly over a long period of time,
changing suddenly

WODWOSE · MANIFESTATION

The Wodwose is the spirit of the woods and as such he has a strong connection with the Green Man. In Celtic legend Merlin went insane following a terrible battle and became the Wild Man of the Woods, during which time he acquired the ability to converse with plants and animals. Later he emerged to become the great wizard of Arthurian legend. Significantly, in these times of environmental ruination, the figure of the Green Man has become prominent once again.

Wodwose combines the practical qualities of Earth with the energy of Fire, hence manifestation. The Earth primary refers to materialism, but the spiritual drive of the Fire element ensures that this is not base. Wodwose therefore refers to social duty, particularly with regard to the environment, both local and global. Wodwose is goal-oriented, a hard-working achiever with high standards. He exhibits technical excellence. He considers physical improvement to be his sacred duty. He is pragmatic and shrewd, ambitious but cautious, and therefore more likely to succeed in the long run. While he appears slow to produce anything, his tenacious efforts are suddenly rewarded with dramatic change. He relies on his senses for information, works to a plan but demands plenty of latitude. He is tough-minded and individualistic, but friendly, with an earthy sense of humor. He not only works hard—he knows how to enjoy himself.

Wodwose reversed refers to inertia. In Greek myth, Cronus, fearing usurpation by his children, devoured them and castrated his father. His wife, the Earth goddess Rhea, managed to save her son Zeus, who returned to overthrow Cronus. Wodwose reversed therefore refers to death rather than life, to stagnation rather than change. There is a lack of ambition or direction and a failure of vision leading to depression and hopelessness. Vitality is lacking and there is a feeling that the spirit is cut off. Consequently there is no faith in anything beyond the physical, and belief is based entirely on immediate sense impressions. There is no respect for the environment, there is waste of resources and interest is strictly limited to short-term gain and profit. Gains are squandered or selfishly hoarded. Inverted Wodwose points to the monotonous pursuit of outmoded and irrelevant goals, and being in a rut.

GRYPHON
Earth and Air

Upright: acquisition, security, stability

Reversed: lack of stability, insecurity, loss of possessions

Direction: north northeast

Time: January, 2 AM

Pace of Change: very slow and gradual

GRYPHON · STABILITY

The Gryphon is half eagle, half lion, and it is small wonder that it has a reputation for being a powerful guardian, not only of earthly treasure but the pathway to spiritual enlightenment. A massive creature, its avian characteristics symbolize the upward journey of the spirit, while its mammalian qualities refer to its earthly nature.

Gryphon is primarily of the Earth and is therefore acquisitive, realistic, and practical. The emphasis is on self-help and security, but the humanitarian qualities associated with the Air element ensure that others are helped and protected too. Gryphon is peaceful and placid as long as his security is not threatened, but he is a ferocious guardian if his stability is compromised. He is reserved, but a good friend and extremely reliable. Because of the objective quality of Air he is also valued for his impartiality. He is known to be knowledgeable and even wise. Gryphon is a good communicator. He is open to new ideas and is intellectually curious, but only interested in theory as long as it has an obvious practical utility. He is a hard worker who looks for tangible results from his efforts. He demonstrates excellent self-discipline and although he likes structure he also needs plenty of autonomy.

Gryphon reversed refers to the beast of Nemesis, the daughter of hell and the night. Nemesis was the goddess of vengeance and Gryphon her instrument of retribution. Clearly there is little stability or security here. Reversed, Gryphon also refers to materialism but in this aspect it is selfish, greedy, and miserly. Insecurity is the basis of an antisocial attitude that is marked by irritability and aggression.

Opinions are biased and unreliable. This beast is self- indulgent and lazy, totally lacking self-discipline. He is also ignorant and closed-minded. When he does act it is for selfish reasons, otherwise he is unpredictable.

PEGASUS
Air and Earth

Upright: idealism, perfectionism, order, fairness

Reversed: chaos, impracticality, misunderstanding

Direction: northeast

Time: February, Brigantia, 4 AM

Pace of Change: rapidly at first, but suddenly
coming to a halt

PEGASUS · TRANSCENDENCE

Pegasus was born from the blood of Medusa in the temple of Artemis, goddess of wisdom. Although born of earthly material, Pegasus eventually became a heavenly constellation. Thus the world of matter was transcended in favor of the world of spirit.

Pegasus is one of the intellectual signifiers, and although the Earth element confers practicality, perfectionism is still a goal. This is associated with the wish to establish order in place of chaos. Because of the humanitarian principle that is a feature of the Air element, Pegasus indicates a striving after worthy goals that may benefit all. He indicates idealism despite being grounded by the Earth secondary. Therefore a desire to produce great ideas that can find practical expression is evident. Pegasus indicates organizational flair. Pegasus highlights original, perhaps idiosyncratic thinking. However there is a need to see results after all the talking is done. Communication is at a premium, but it will surround practical tasks. Impartiality and scrupulous fairness are paramount. Creativity, especially involving language, is prominent.

Pegasus reversed refers to the nightmare. In Celtic myth, the goddess sometimes took this form attended by nine horrendous fillies. This aspect of Pegasus is the bringer of chaos, confusion, and the inability to transcend the physical. Faith may be absent and ideals cast aside, or there is the impractical idealism of the dreamer who has no impact on the world. Cut off from others by misunderstandings, there is an inability to communicate effectively, or you may be the recipient of mixed messages. Creativity is blocked and there is a lack of originality.

UNICORN
Air and Water

Upright: knowledge, wisdom, understanding

Reversed: stupidity, rigidity, lack of imagination

Direction: east

Time: March, spring equinox, 6 AM

Pace of Change: rapid at first, slowing gradually

UNICORN · PURITY

The Unicorn is one of the most familiar of all fabulous beasts. It combines the head and body of a horse with the legs of a deer and the tail of a lion, but its defining feature is the single horn emerging from its forehead. This horn suggests the unity of all creation, and this, along with the beast's whiteness, is a symbol of purity.

The appearance of Unicorn not only indicates purity of thought, but wisdom and understanding. Unicorn points to knowledge from diverse areas and to penetrating insight. This is not only relevant to the world of ideas, because the Water secondary relates to feelings. Comprehension therefore extends to the deepest needs of self and others, coupled with the ability to communicate these realizations. Unicorn signals social activities, talk, and laughter. Travel or communication with foreigners is possible. This may mean communication with Otherworld entities. If so, the primary Air confers the necessary discrimination. Artistic activities are highlighted, as is the world of the imagination generally. Unicorn emphasizes the importance of the unconventional and the eccentric, the individualist. Air and Water means that reason is allied with feelings, hence altruism and compassion.

Unicorns were believed to be extremely dangerous creatures who could only be captured by a virgin. Unicorn reversed warns of impure thoughts or feelings. Beware of obtuseness, inability to understand, and intellectual aridity. There is also a threat of boring, suffocating convention and intellectual rigidity. As well as a lack of imagination there can be a total lack of insight. Misanthropy and prejudice can be a problem. Reason is divorced from feeling, leading to emotional insensitivity on the one hand and oversensitivity on the other. Exchanges can be motivated by spite, while problems with travel hinder progress. There can be a preoccupation with the Otherworld and its denizens or fear of the same.

FIREBIRD
Air and Fire

Upright: humanitarian, achieving, innovation

Reversed: obstruction, discord, ignorance

Direction: southeast

Time: April, 8 AM

Pace of Change: rapid, becoming faster

FIREBIRD · REFORMATION

The Firebird of Russian myth helps to defeat evil. It has some similarity with the Native American Thunderbird that also defeats evil. The combination of human and avian reflects the marriage of Air and Fire that is found in this beast.

Firebird therefore refers to reforming, revolutionary zeal, and a drive to overcome injustice. Firebird usually shows up when there is a strong desire to achieve something of social importance. Air relates to humanitarian interests and to moral and ethical imperatives, while Fire relates to spiritual matters, hence the focus on justice. In addition Firebird is the sign of the ingenious innovator who is constantly looking for new challenges. A rich source of ideas and a problem-solver, Firebird is indicative of contagious enthusiasm, one that inspires others to greater efforts.

Firebird reversed is a bird of prey and an omen of bad fortune. In Native American myth, children were taken up by a great bird and devoured. Far from improving things, Firebird reversed warns that matters will not improve and indeed may get worse. It may be that someone is obstructing progress, either out of stupidity or deliberately for selfish reasons. This aspect suggests specious arguments used to maintain the status quo or simply ignorance and bigotry. Moral or ethical standards are compromised. It may be that double standards lead to injustice. Beware of self-serving motives. Firebird reversed also signals inability to progress due to lack of vision and lack of ideas.

DRAGON
Fire and Air

Upright: enthusiasm, charisma, urgency

Reversed: arrogance, aggression, force

Direction: south southeast

Time: May, Beltane, 10 AM

Pace of Change: very fast and sustained

DRAGON · TRANSFORMATION

Dragons are probably the most familiar of all the fabulous beasts. They appear in myth and folklore from various parts of the world; in the Orient they were regarded as good omens, in the West they were associated with destruction. In the East and the West they were regarded as the vital spirits of Earth, Water, and the weather.

With Fire as the primary element, key words for Dragon are energetic, enthusiastic, expansiveness, boldness, and fearlessness. The secondary Air confers a rational aspect so that the awesome power associated with Dragon has direction. This combination of idea and drive leads to transformation. Dragon therefore represents moving swiftly toward a goal, a love of challenge, and a need to move forward to completion. Dragon signals optimism and open-mindedness. Self-confidence has reached a peak and vitality pushes one on to success. Dragon heralds a creative upsurge. It may indicate personal transformation or the arrival of someone with great charisma that inspires others to new heights. Dragon is concerned with the broad sweep, not the details, and after the flare of initial interest moves on to new projects. Dragon is the visionary leader with deep spiritual motives and a view of a better future.

Dragon reversed refers to the destructive power of unreasoned force or the extinction of the life force and the triumph of death. Reversed, Dragon therefore means change for the worse or complete inertia. The negative power of Fire can mean arrogance, aggression, an overbearing attitude, and an urge to dominate and enslave others for selfish ends. Dragon reversed often signals the appearance of the coldhearted psychopath. If the power of Fire is not destructive it is absent, and lethargy reigns. There is lack of interest and enthusiasm, lack of confidence, and lack of faith in one's own efforts. Sometimes it is not the absence of power so much as the lack of direction. Frequently there is a fear of change, fear of the future.

PHOENIX
Fire and Earth

Upright: revolution, change, optimism

Reversed: stagnation, inhibition, pessimism

Direction: south

Time: June, summer solstice, midday

Pace of Change: very rapid, slowing gradually

PHOENIX · REBIRTH

Most people are familiar with the legend of the phoenix, the magnificent bird that is consumed in a fire of its own making and that rises anew from the ashes. The phoenix does not therefore die, but is transformed and reborn in a continuous cycle of change.

Phoenix is the process of evolution and revolution. The Fire primary suggests the revolutionary change through conflagration, while the Earth secondary refers to the more gradual evolution. Phoenix therefore indicates gradual development that suddenly reaches a crescendo of spectacular change. Initial appearances are therefore deceptive because nothing seems to be happening until the spectacular transformation capitalizes on the groundwork. At this point the caution and deliberation of Earth is rewarded in the crucible of change. Phoenix signals that great change rewards patient optimism. This bird is a sign that matters are about to reach a conclusion, as long as impatience doesn't short-circuit the process.

Phoenix reversed means the failure of the process of transformation as the bird is consumed without reemerging. Here the process ends in death or stagnation. There may be a failure of nerve that inhibits change at the crucial moment. Pessimism and lack of faith produce the same dampening effect—otherwise there is a danger that the heat will become too intense and the change taken too far. Mania and grandiosity may take the place of vibrancy and realism. Phoenix reversed may warn of sluggishness and a failure to evolve. Lack of staying power and lack of foresight undermine the process.

WYVERN
Fire and Water

Upright: courage, a champion, tenacity

Reversed: opposition, cowardice, threat

Direction: south southwest

Time: July, 2 PM

Pace of Change: very rapid, cooling rapidly

WYVERN · JUSTICE

The Wyvern is the mid-stage of the development of the dragon. In myth, dragons are born in the sea and gradually develop forelegs and wings before developing into dragons proper. The Wyvern was a common heraldic emblem in medieval times because it was regarded as more ferocious even than the dragon.

Wyvern signals the power of justice. In its positive aspect this is to be welcomed because it shows that your aims are true and that opposition will be overcome. Wyvern indicates great courage, either in the face of a personal adversary or as a defender of the weak. The appearance of this beast may indicate that a champion is about to appear or that you are about to take on this role yourself. This is most likely to be on behalf of a group or against an authority. While it can refer to lawsuits, it may refer to a less formal dispute requiring tenacity and strength. Either way there is a power at hand that is driven by moral convictions to uphold the good. This empowers others and encourages them to rally to a cause. Wyvern marks the appearance of the admirable leader, whether the spirit of this beast manifests in someone familiar to you, including yourself, or a stranger who acts as a unifying force. In any event this is a force that will prevail.

Wyvern reversed stands for the destructiveness of war and the triumph of injustice. The appearance of this aspect of Wyvern thus warns of powerful opposition that cannot be overcome directly. It also means a powerful enemy and hence the need for a champion. Wyvern reversed means being disempowered or being threatened by malevolent forces. This beast suggests that support is lacking and that allies are divided. Wyvern reversed means cowardice in the face of a challenge or undue ferocity and uncontrollable rage. Beware also dubious moralizing.

CHIMERA
Water and Fire

Upright: originality, intimacy, desire

Reversed: fear, nightmares, estrangement

Direction: southwest

Time: August, Lughnassagh, 4 PM

Pace of Change: slow, developing gradually

CHIMERA · IMAGINATION

The Chimera is a composite beast consisting of lion, goat, and dragon. In the beginning she was the divine daughter of the storm god Typhon and the snake goddess Echidne. Chimera originally ruled the sky as the sun and the moon but succeeding cultures demonized her. Today her name is a byword for fantastic imaginings.

Chimera represents the combined power of the dreamy aspect of Water and the urgency of Fire, hence the imagination and the creative impulse. Chimera therefore indicates the startlingly original. Inspiration is derived from myth, dreams, and the occult, and a new, radically different and exciting creation emerges. Future possibilities can be envisaged with optimism. Also indicated by this beast is the intimacy of shared experience and chance encounters. The Water primary suggests emotional desire, the Fire suggests secondary passion. Chimera thus indicates security through a close intimate bond. You may be aware of increased passion and compassion giving rise to cooperative endeavors, whether in the artistic or occult realms. Chimera brings the worlds together to enhance the communication. Messages from spirit are more easily received. A telepathic link seems to develop between those who feel an affinity with each other. The power of group work is enhanced.

Chimera reversed refers to the fire-breathing monster that terrorized the ancient world until Bellerophon killed it. In modern parlance, the chimera is a product of a fevered imagination, which accurately describes the effect of Fire being out of balance with Water. Chimera reversed therefore warns of lurid fears, nightmares and a sense of not being on control. The appearance of this beast may refer to separation, estrangement, discord, and lack of understanding among people. The breakup of a close relationship may be central to these experiences. Alternatively Chimera may indicate a rift between the worlds that hinders creativity.

MERMAID
Water and Air

Upright: dreams, unconventional, perceptive

Reversed: bizarre, moody, irrational

Direction: west

Time: September, autumn equinox, 6 PM

Pace of Change: slow, developing very gradually

MERMAID · REVELATION

Mermaids are among the most easily recognized of the fabulous beasts. They are typically portrayed as beautiful young women with the tails of fish, although mermen are also referred to. They combine the unconscious with the conscious, the occult with the known. Like dream symbols, they swim in the depths and bring treasures to the surface.

Mermaid connects with the deep unconscious, hence dreams, intuition, and a profound connection with the Otherworld. Mermaid is fey, unworldly, psychic, and deeply spiritual. Mermaid refers to the unusual and unconventional, to synchronicity and being in tune with the time. Mermaid confers an ability to quickly understand complex problems. She is intensely curious, and her ability to be both perceptive and objective makes her a wise counselor or inspiring teacher. The appearance of this beast thus indicates both revelation and enhanced understanding. Mermaid is also creative by virtue of the Water and Air combination, especially in the realms of music and song. Mermaid expresses deep concern for all life and she cares passionately for others. Nevertheless she is elusive and difficult to pin down.

Mermaid reversed refers to the destructive sirens of Greek myth or the German Lorelei. These creatures would sing to sailors, luring them to their deaths on the rocks. In folklore there are numerous tales about mermaids who temporarily grow legs so that they can come ashore to seduce the unwary before leading them into the sea to drown. Mermaid reversed thus refers to drowning in the depths of the unconscious or being lost in the Otherworld. This aspect of Mermaid warns of bizarre and unsubstantiated ideas, an inability to tell fact from fantasy, and loss of reason. Alternatively, beware of emotional unpredictability, touchiness, and moodiness. There is a possibility of emotional distance and coldness. This presentation of Mermaid may indicate disconnection from the familiar element and hence being divorced from the secrets of the worlds beyond. Sometimes it may refer to unyielding skepticism.

SATYR
Water and Earth

Upright: union, passion, pleasure

Reversed: excess, impotence, debauchery

Direction: northwest

Time: October, 8 PM

Pace of Change: slow, coming to a halt

SATYR · UNION

The Satyr is closely associated with the Greek nature god Pan, although versions of this woodland creature can be found in Russia and in Britain. Easily recognized because of his human torso and shaggy goat's legs and horns, the Satyr combines the passion of Water with the delights of the physical.

Satyr is a sociable beast that craves union with others through physical intimacy. Satyr has a deep understanding of the realm of the Otherworld by virtue of the Water primary. This quality also confers deep passion and desire that seeks expression in the physical by virtue of the secondary Earth element. Satyr thus represents seduction and sexual pleasure. Satyr indicates a time of sharing with others, communing with nature, and enjoying the experience of untamed wildness. Satyr may mean hedonism, but the Earth component brings caution rather than excess. Earth also means that desires may be fulfilled, since Earth is the element of material manifestation. The Water primary suggests that these will be shared or attained in cooperation with others. Water also refers to the occult and the hidden realm of the dead. Be prepared for someone who is enigmatic, mysterious, and charming. He or she may be a musician or performing artist.

Satyr reversed refers to the uncontrolled rapine of the bestial. The passion of the Water element and the physicality of Earth warns of the sexual predator who is looking for conquests. The desire to experience intimacy and connection with another is rejected in favor of rapaciousness. Alternatively, this beast warns of impotence, rejection, and lack of commitment. Reversed, Satyr may signal rejection of the world of the senses and consequently a dour, joyless outlook. Or the sensual pull of the Earth element may lead to overindulgence. This beast often warns of a fear of death arising from a lack of faith in anything beyond the physical.

COW
Earth • Water • Fire • Air

Upright: wealth, possessions, money

Reversed: poverty, loss, misanthropy

Direction: 316–350 degrees

Time: early November, 1–2 PM

Pace of Change: very slow, as in the steady
accumulation of wealth

COW · WEALTH

The number of cows possessed used to indicate the wealth of a family and, in many parts of the world, this is still the case. Thus Cow represents possessions, goods, and even money. The rune Feoh, which means wealth, is associated with Cow. Cow also refers to generosity and security, hospitality, and the spirit of welcome. Cow is conscientious and attentive to the wellbeing of self and others. Cow is very family-centered and likes to include friends as part of the family. Cow regards everyone as part of one big family. Consequently her inexhaustible supply of milk nourishes all. Hers is the milk of human kindness as much as real mother's milk. Cow signals the appearance of the Mother Goddess and her loving attention. Cow also represents spiritual riches. In Celtic myth, cattle are gifts of the goddess and the wealth of the people are tied to the wellbeing of these animals. Neighboring tribes would sometimes try to steal this divine favor, as in the Cattle raid of Cooley.

Cow reversed alerts one to poverty and need, both earthly and spiritual. There may be a crisis in one or both respects. There may be neglect of self or others in some sense. Sometimes it indicates someone who gives but cannot receive in return. There may be problems with mothers or children. Cow reversed is antisocial and miserly, selfish and misanthropic. Alternatively, she may indicate the pain of isolation and a yearning to be part of a family or to find good friends. Perhaps there is difficulty with family or friends.

SOW
Earth · Water · Air · Fire

Upright: fertility, nurture, sustenance

Reversed: infertility, selfishness, greediness

Direction: 331–345 degrees

Time: late November, 2–3 PM

Pace of Change: slow, as befits gentle nurturing

SOW · NURTURE

Sow is most closely associated with fertility and birth, hence nurture. Sow is extremely protective of her young. Fertility and children are among the gifts of the Earth Goddess. Sow is most closely associated with Cerridwen and the Crone aspect of the goddess, hence the past and reincarnation. Sow therefore not only indicates matters connected with childbirth and the young, but also ancestry and the elders. Adults care for children and the elderly. The elderly may care for both, and the ancestral spirits care for the living as well as those as yet unborn. Sow also refers to the inception and nurturing of new projects.

Sow reversed may indicate infertility. This aspect of Sow is the Dark Goddess who devours her own offspring. Sow reversed warns of lack of support or failure to support others. Consequently there is a lack of security and a sense of want. Sow reversed also relates to greediness, hoarding, and self-indulgence. There may also be problems connected with inheritance in some sense, or disturbing associations with the family past.

HORSE
Earth • Fire • Water • Air

Upright: movement, freedom, stamina

Reversed: blockages, constraints, weakness

Direction: 346–360 degrees

Time: early December, 11 PM–12 AM

Pace of Change: constant, as when reserves are high
and movement unfettered

HORSE · POWER

Horse instantly conjures up images of swift movement across the face of the Earth, ease of travel, energy, stamina, and freedom. This freedom and lack of restraint permits exploration, both of this world and the Otherworld. In the Mabinogian story "Pwyll Lord of Dyved," Pwyll chases Rhiannon but is unable to catch her until he bids her stop. She then berates him for not doing so earlier "for the sake of your horse." Horse evokes a sense of enthusiasm, nobility, grace, hope, and confidence. Horse represents the Goddess herself and the land on which Horse runs. Horse is therefore indicative of power and the ability to bring change to whatever area is being worked on.

Horse reversed indicates weakness, slowness, lethargy, and constraint. Perhaps you are overburdened and used as a cart horse, as it were. You may feel powerless and dispossessed. You may be restless and yearning to escape or to progress, but are restrained by something. Horse reversed also warns of abuse of power and trampling on the rights of others. There may be signs of wildness and irresponsibility. You may lack confidence and hope. Horse reversed may indicate a need to regain respect for the Goddess, and to reconnect with the spirit and the land.

BEAR
Earth • Fire • Air • Water

Upright: protection, strength, introspection

Reversed: aggression, cowardice, anger

Direction: 1–15 degrees

Time: late December, 12–1 AM

Pace of Change: very slow to start, becoming active
suddenly; vigilance leads to protection

BEAR · PROTECTION

Bear represents protection, particularly of a mother for her cubs. There is no more fierce defender of the weak and needy than Bear. Bear is strength and courage in the face of threat and the sure sense of prevailing against the odds. Bear commands respect for this. Bear is patient, alert, and watchful. Thus Bear also refers to self-analysis and inner awareness, to connection with self. In this sense, Bear can refer to self-discovery through introspection, dreams, and sensitive use of intuition. The name Arthur is derived from the word "art," meaning bear.

Bear reversed warns of danger and may indicate failure to protect others, cowardice, or even aggression from those who should be protective. This aspect of Bear is the fierce mother who is excessively punitive; alternatively it is over-protection and smother-love that does not permit development in the young, anger and aggression that is vengeful and uncontrolled. Bear reversed also urges self-examination to develop self-knowledge and personal insight.

DOG
Earth • Air • Water • Fire

Upright: devotion, protection, guidance

Reversed: deceit, enemies, fear

Direction: 16–30 degrees

Time: early January, 1–2 AM

Pace of Change: slow to start, gradually warming as if developing attachment

DOG · LOYALTY

In Celtic myth, Dog is most closely associated with Cu Chulainn, "the hound of Chulainn." The keyword for Dog is loyalty. Dogs are believed to be the first domesticated animals and have been companions of humans since the earliest times. They would have been valued for their devotion, friendship, and allegiance to the tribe because of their warning and protective functions. As well as guardians, they would have become valued as hunting companions. Being pack animals, social relationships and rules are of great importance to them. Dog also represents the guardian of the entrance to the Otherworld, the realm of the dead and the secrets that lie beyond. Dog therefore signals the closeness of the Otherworld and guides those who enter this realm.

Dog reversed indicates disloyalty, deceit, an enemy, and possible attack. There may be mistrust of others, social exclusion, or an outsider. Dog reversed also refers to ignoring social rules and traditions and antisocial behavior. This aspect of Dog refers to the underdog and an inability to act independently. Folklore is replete with tales of phantom black dogs that haunt byways and mislead travelers. Depression is sometimes described as a black dog. There may be a morbid fascination with death, a fear of death, or inability to adapt to loss. Dog reversed can refer to unquiet spirits.

CAT
Earth • Air • Fire • Water

Upright: the occult, clairvoyance, decisiveness

Reversed: skepticism, obstacles, secrets

Direction: 31–45 degrees

Time: late January, 2–3 AM

Pace of Change: slow to start, gradually gaining pace
until moving forward suddenly

CAT · PSYCHIC

Cat is the animal most closely associated with psychic ability and is commonly regarded as an ally of the occultist, as the perennial image of the witch and her black cat amply illustrates. Black cats in particular are associated with good luck; cats are probably the most popular of earthly familiars. Cat has a fully deserved reputation for being in touch with the Otherworld, and indeed they often seem to be meditating. Cat is thus associated with clairvoyance and magic. Cat is notoriously curious, not only about this world but also the next. Cat loves to discover the answer to secrets but she is also enigmatic. She is swift and decisive in her actions but does not act rashly. Cat is also associated with sensuality, pride, and female energy. Cat is extremely perceptive and not easily fooled.

Cat reversed suggests a lack of psychic ability or rejection of these gifts due to fear or skepticism. Cat reversed can indicate bad luck or unseen obstacles to success. She can indicate a poor link with the Otherworld and its forces or being overly cautious and timid in connection with these. Cat can represent closed-mindedness and a limited range of interests. She may be too secretive or alternatively warns of being kept in the dark about something. She may be sexually seductive, or one who preys on females and disparages them.

WREN
Air • Earth • Water • Fire

Upright: resourcefulness, wit, confidence

Reversed: dourness, trickery, ineffectual

Direction: 46–60 degrees

Time: early February, 3–4 AM

Pace of Change: very gradual, as befits cautious optimism

WREN · CONFIDENCE

Wren is another creature that features prominently in Celtic myth, having a close connection to the Druids and to the god Bran. The story of how Wren rode on Eagle's back to the greatest height and then flew higher still to become the greatest of birds is a tale told by the Native Americans as well as the Celts. This story illustrates Wren's cleverness and resourcefulness as well as demonstrating a wry sense of humor. Wren is subtle and gentle for the most part, but can be fearless in defense. Such confidence and boldness is so unexpected in such a small bird that it takes aggressors by surprise. Wren is a loud, cheerful bird that wants to live life to the fullest. Wren also has a reputation for being a messenger from the gods and for prophecy, hence the connection with Bran.

Wren reversed refers to lack of confidence, lack of a sense of humor, no sense of fun, and dourness. This bird can warn of trickery, theft, and plagiarism. Wren reversed can mean being too humble and obsequious, shyness, lacking courage of convictions, poor self-belief. Associated with these is feeling unable to cope, feeling ineffectual, overwhelmed, and small next to the competition. It may indicate that resources are in short supply or that they are not being used wisely. There may be a lack of assertiveness and being victimized as a result; or alternatively being aggressive, bullying those weaker than oneself, indicating a need to pay attention to messages from spirit.

OWL
Air • Earth • Fire • Water

Upright: knowledge, perception, insight

Reversed: deception, ignorance, darkness

Direction: 61–75 degrees

Time: late February, 4–5 AM

Pace of Change: gradual, as when receiving and acting on occult information

OWL · OMENS

In Celtic myth, Blodeuwedd, the woman made of flowers, was transformed into an owl by Gwydion. Owl was the bird of the Greek goddess Athena and acted as guardian of the Acropolis. Owl is universally associated with wisdom and knowledge, largely because this twilight creature of the threshold is recognized as having access to secrets and to esoteric lore. This knowledge also confers objectivity and impartiality. Owl also represents the silence of the wise, those who watch and listen but who keep their own counsel. Owl is also gifted with the ability to see the invisible and is associated with exceptional powers of insight. Owl has great powers of perception and cannot be deceived. Owl is an astral traveler and a powerful guide to the Otherworld. He brings messages from the deep unconscious, often in the form of dreams or flashes of intuition. He is the bird of omens and is associated with the moon, hence clairvoyance and the psychic realms. Owl also represents solitude and those pursuits that will encourage the development of psychic abilities, such as meditation.

Owl is regarded as a bad omen in many cultures, one that brings unwanted changes and who is sometimes a harbinger of death. Owl is also associated with deception and mistrust. Information is distorted, hidden from others, or unpleasant and damaging secrets are revealed. There may be deception of self and others, or deceit by others. Owl reversed means lack of wisdom and a need to develop understanding. Most obviously this bird means ignorance, but also being seduced by the lure of the dark side, tempted by black magic, or failure to connect with the Otherworld and a need for guidance.

SALMON
Air • Water • Earth • Fire

Upright: wisdom, inspiration, eloquence

Reversed: obtuseness, closed-mindedness,
inarticulateness

Direction: 76–90 degrees

Time: early March, 5–6 AM

Pace of change: slow, as befits developing wisdom

SALMON · WISDOM

In Celtic myth Salmon is the oldest of all the animals and is consequently associated with great wisdom. Salmon inhabits the depths of the enchanted pool where he lives on the fruit of the tree of wisdom itself. Gwion was given the task of minding the cauldron of Cerridwen in which was being cooked the great salmon of wisdom. He accidentally tasted the brew after it scalded his thumb, and after being devoured by Cerridwen he was reborn as the great bard Taliesin. The Celts reverenced Water particularly, because lakes and ponds were regarded as entry points to the Otherworld. Reference to sacred pools and water spirits are found throughout the Celtic lands. Salmon lives in these waters and therefore has occult knowledge and recall of ancient traditions and oral culture. Salmon conveys inspiration, eloquence, and creative ability, especially with respect to poetry and rhetoric. Salmon also refers to divination and to divine utterance. Such deep wisdom confers knowledge of past, present, and future, and of past lives. Salmon represents the personal quest and insight. Salmon means openness to new experiences and ideas.

Salmon reversed suggests stupidity, tactlessness, and being too forthright and outspoken. Verbal aggression, spiteful wit, and sarcasm are also suggested. At the same time the perpetrator may display oversensitivity. Salmon reversed indicates blocks to creativity and to an inability to communicate effectively. Beware lack of understanding or the uncritical acceptance of the opinions of others, closed-mindedness, and a refusal to listen. This fish warns against a selective memory and forgetfulness. Reversed Salmon also warns against shallowness and being cut off from the unconscious and from the Otherworld of spirit.

CRANE
Air • Water • Fire • Earth

Upright: longevity, ancient lore, vigilance

Reversed: impatience, distortion, carelessness

Direction: 91–105 degrees

Time: late March, 6–7 AM

Pace of Change: slow, as befits one who watches and waits

CRANE · LONGEVITY

Crane is especially important in Celtic mythology as the guardian of Annwn, the underworld. Manannan mac Lir made a bag of the crane's skin in which to keep magical objects, a practice that has a parallel in the medicine bundle of the Native Americans. Crane was also held to be sacred by various ancient cultures including the Greeks and the Chinese. Crane represents longevity and past lives. The contents of the crane bag include the lore of one's culture carried over from generation to generation. This wisdom is often jealously guarded and kept secret, away from the uninitiated. Crane also represents magic, the occult, and access to the Otherworld. Crane represents past, present, and future and is associated with the Norns of Viking myth, particularly Erda, the crone aspect. Crane also refers to creativity due to the links with intelligence and disciplined ability to maintain focus. Vigilance, concentration, and patience are key characteristics of this bird.

Crane reversed indicates shortsightedness and impatience; careless and inaccurate observation, poor concentration, and prejudice, ignoring important information because it doesn't fit with preformed ideas, distorting information for the same reason, hiding unpalatable facts; failure to learn from past mistakes, failure to listen to wise council; self-isolation, forsaking others, mistrust of others, misanthropy; a need to be alone but unable to find time or space, being pressured by others. Crane reversed can indicate a complaining attitude, harshness, and faultfinding. This bird urges you to pay attention to the lore and wisdom of elders and ancestors.

FOX
Air • Fire • Earth • Water

Upright: intelligence, slyness, watchfulness

Reversed: imprudence, haste, unobservant

Direction: 106–120 degrees

Time: early April, 7–8 AM

Pace of Change: swift, as befits the quick thinking of the survivor

FOX · INTELLIGENCE

Fox is universally associated with quick-wittedness, slyness, and cunning, as well as the intelligence demanded of an animal that has a reputation for being a champion survivor. Legends abound of Fox's adaptability and wily nature, from China throughout Europe and in the United States. Associated with this swiftness of thought and a surefootedness born of wise caution is the ability to move silently and unseen. Instead of being seen, Fox is the keen observer and watcher. All Fox's senses are acute—hearing and smell as well as sight. In addition, Fox has the reputation for being fiercely protective of the family; they use their natural cunning to good effect.

Fox reversed means slow-wittedness, uncertainty, indecision and imprudence. Fox reversed warns of an inability to adapt when necessary and of consequent danger. Fox represents poor coordination, poor powers of perception, and failure to be aware of threats and potential danger. Alternatively, the skills of the Fox can be used to the disadvantage of others. Fox can use intelligence to undermine others. There can also be a failure to protect others close to oneself.

EAGLE
Air • Fire • Water • Earth

Upright: vision, expansion, objectivity

Reversed: shortsightedness, skepticism, sterile thinking

Direction: 121–135 degrees

Time: late April, 8–9 AM

Pace of Change: fast, in accordance with direct perception and sudden awareness

EAGLE · VISION

Eagle is featured in the story "Culhwch and Olwen" as one of the oldest and wisest of birds. Eagle is universally associated with spirit, expansiveness, vision, and farsightedness. These ideas obviously derive from the image of the eagle soaring majestically high in the sky, with the best possible view of the ground extending for many miles. Eagles are famous for their keen eyesight. Flying so high also suggests being closer to the Divine, so the idea of expansion and insight extends to spiritual matters. Thus, Eagle refers to connection with spirit and with guidance. Eagle has insight and is able to penetrate beyond the veil of illusion that cloaks the Otherworld. Eagle therefore represents truth, a spiritual test, and being able to see the underlying reality of the Otherworld hidden in appearances. This naturally confers great wisdom and objectivity. Eagle is astute, purposeful, decisive, and self-directed. Eagle also represents freedom, strength, power, and fearlessness.

Eagle reversed suggests shortsightedness, poor insight, often associated with overreliance on materialism and a failure to transcend the lure of the earthly; intellectual aridity with associated disconnection from spirit due to skepticism; also sterile thought patterns, lack of imagination; a focus on the petty and low at the expense of higher ideals; lack of refinement; frustration at not making progress toward intellectual or spiritual goals, or lack of opportunity to do so. This bird may indicate failure to recognize a guide or to heed one when she or he appears. Eagle reversed may refer to a sense of powerlessness; alternatively, beware of using power for destructive ends. Eagle reversed may mean lack of warmth, emotional distance, and lack of sympathy. Sometimes it can even mean savagery and aggression.

BLACKBIRD
Fire • Air • Water • Earth

Upright: guidance, balance, revelation

Reversed: passivity, naivete, pessimism

Direction: 131–150 degrees

Time: early May, 9–10 AM

Pace of Change: very fast, as if making
an important discovery

BLACKBIRD · GUIDE

In the Mabinogian tale "Culhwch and Olwen," Blackbird is the first of the most ancient animals approached by King Arthur's men in their search for the lost child Mabon. This myth indicates that Blackbird was regarded by the Celts as one of the wisest and most spiritual of animals. Blackbird calls us to spiritual quests and guides us to the hidden entrance to the Otherworld where occult knowledge and wisdom can be accessed. Blackbird is therefore associated with active attempts to follow spirit, hence pathworking, journeying, meditation, and trance. However, Blackbird also relates to the balance between the spiritual and the mundane and the need to remain grounded in this world of matter. Blackbird may appear as a guide or herald the arrival of a guide.

Reversed, Blackbird refers to a need to pursue the spiritual, but not knowing the way and needing guidance. This aspect of Blackbird may be a sign of fear of proceeding, of being deaf to the call and blind to the signs. Sometimes there is a passive expectation that the spiritual will come to you rather than having to go in search of it. Blackbird reversed may indicate pessimism over finding the way, or even rejection of the world of spirit. Sometimes there is a danger of renouncing this world in favor of the Otherworld; alternatively, the spiritual may be rejected in favor of the mundane world. In either event a lack of balance is the result. Beware also of following false guides who may be working for their own ends.

STAG
Fire • Air • Earth • Water

Upright: independence, potency, strength

Reversed: recklessness, arrogance, impotence

Direction: 151–165 degrees

Time: late May, 10–11 AM

Pace of Change: very fast, as with controlled passion

STAG · CHANGE

In the Mabinogian, the search for the lost child Mabon leads King Arthur's men to Blackbird, who directs them to an even older animal, Stag. In Celtic myth, Stag is associated with the Lord of the Underworld, so it's no surprise that this animal confers a deep understanding of the cycle of life, death, and rebirth. Stag also naturally facilitates communication with the dead and acts as a guide to those exploring the ancestral realms. Purification is an aspect of this process. On a more mundane level, Stag is associated with independence, pride, majesty, and nobility. An obviously male symbol, Stag represents virility, potency, wildness, and strength. The appearance of this animal indicates a balance between power and self-control; Stag is a mighty adversary but he does not act rashly. His actions are considered and purposeful. Stage indicates that there are many paths to a goal.

Stag reversed suggests fear of death or more generally of change. If this animal has appeared there is a danger of ignoring issues connected with death and dying. Stag reversed may warn against a reckless, death-defying attitude. Maybe you are ignoring communications from those who have gone before. Perhaps you or someone close to you is unable to come to terms with the loss of a loved one. Stag may suggest failure to honor the ancestors. On a more mundane level, this aspect of Stag can indicate excessive pride and arrogance. There is a risk of chauvinism and a glorification of the worst aspects of maleness. Alternatively, this animal reversed can indicate disparaging the male sex and the qualities associated with it. Stag reversed refers to impotence, weakness, and dependency, or poor self-control and ill-considered actions.

BOAR
Fire • Earth • Air • Water

Upright: courage, tenacity, leadership

Reversed: destructiveness, weakness, cowardice

Direction: 166–180 degrees

Time: early June, 11–12 noon

Pace of Change: swift but measured, as befits
a skilled warrior

BOAR · STRENGTH

In Celtic legend, Boar possesses great strength and he is consequently respected as the warrior spirit: fearless, courageous, indefatigable, and tenacious. Boar moves swiftly and with great confidence to overcome problems or protect against attack. Boar shows impressive leadership qualities with clear aims and direction, inspiring others with displays of fierceness and energy. Boar is terrifying and indispensable when faced with powerful opposition or a threat. However, beyond mere physical strength lies magical power. In myth, both Arthur and the hero Culhwch hunt the mystical boar in order to obtain talismans of power with which to overcome their adversaries.

Boar reversed can represent wanton displays of destructiveness, aggression, warmongering, blood lust, and savagery. Boar in this position can be cruel and vindictive, brutish, mad. The strength and endurance that could serve self and others so well is perverted and used to oppress those who are weaker. Such behavior is frequently self-defeating. Alternatively, reversed Boar can mean weakness, cowardice, lack of staying power, vacillation, loss of direction, and poor leadership.

SNAKE
Fire • Earth • Water • Air

Upright: energy, passion, initiation

Reversed: lethargy, depression, mania

Direction: 181–195 degrees

Time: late June, 12–1 PM

Pace of Change: fast then stopping immediately,
as in the efficient use of energy reserves

SNAKE · ENERGY

Snakes are probably the most maligned creatures in the world, yet at the same time they are greatly respected by cultures across the globe. In Britain there are only three types of snake: the grass snake, the smooth snake that is only found in a tiny part of Sussex, and the adder, the only venomous snake in the UK. Ireland is famous for having no snakes at all.

This is the animal most directly associated with Fire, hence the life force itself. Consequently Snake represents energy, especially sexual energy, virility, and passion. Snake is associated with charisma, seduction, and procreation. As well as generation, Snake also represents transformation and regeneration. Snake is also associated with ambition, new beginnings, change, and healing. Snakes are valued as effective guardians of treasures. These treasures may be esoteric in nature and Snake is a symbol of initiation into this world of occult knowledge. Snake vigorously overcomes obstacles, doing so decisively and with lightning speed.

Reversed, Snake represents Fire that has died down, and so naturally indicates coldness, slowness, and lack of energy and enthusiasm. There may be a profound need for rest and recuperation. Sometimes it can indicate lethargy, depression, and even fear of life itself. The bite of reversed Snake is the venomous belief in death as an absolute end. Reversed Snake may indicate a need to regenerate, to heal. Otherwise Snake reversed may relate to energy that is out of control like a wildfire, hence mania, being overambitious and lacking in discrimination. There may be a lack of inspiration and creative blocks. It may indicate an aggressor or a victim of spite or vengeance. It can be a sign of sexual inhibition or of being oversexed.

WOLF
Fire • Water • Air • Earth

Upright: learning, communication, sharing

Reversed: hoarding, miscommunication, isolation

Direction: 196–210 degrees

Time: early July, 1–2 PM

Pace of Change: gradual, as in the discovery and assimilation of knowledge

WOLF · TEACHER

Wolf is recognized as a teacher and pathfinder in many traditions, one who crosses the threshold between the worlds and brings back occult knowledge to share with others. Wolf shows a strong urge to enter the Otherworld in order to acquire this knowledge. Wolf is therefore associated with communication and dissemination of spiritual learning. Wolf is also associated with developing self-knowledge. This demands keeping a careful balance between being the lone wolf who takes the risk to cultivate intuition and search the depths for understanding, and the loyal mate and pack member. Although Wolf often works alone, the fruit of that work is always shared. That is the purpose for Wolf, not selfish gain of arcane material for the sake of it. Wolf shows courage both as an individual and as a member of a pack. Wolf is a powerful guardian and guide. Wolf also refers to those community structures that give cohesion to group life, hence the rules and protocols that make effective teamwork possible. Wolf is the free spirit within the group home.

Wolf reversed shows a need to pursue spiritual activities and to acquire knowledge and understanding of the Otherworld. On the other hand he may suggest failure to take advantage of available opportunities to do so. Reversed, Wolf is indicative of fear of the occult. There may be a need for privacy. You may be feeling too crowded and unable to follow your chosen path. Sometimes what is indicated is a fear of being alone or of being introspective, or fear of using your power of intuition. Reversed, Wolf warns of a narrow outlook, of selfishness and hoarding information. He may warn of poor social integration and an inability to live and work harmoniously with others. Consequent upon this is a failure to communicate.

HARE
Fire • Water • Earth • Air

Upright: rebirth, transformation, change

Reversed: procrastination, stagnation, rut

Direction: 211–225 degrees

Time: late July, 2–3 PM

Pace of Change: sudden then steady, in keeping with
a rebirth

HARE · PROMISE

Hare was associated with the moon goddess Andraste and was therefore sacred to the Celts. The common rabbit was not native to Britain but was imported by the Romans. The tradition of the Easter bunny and the connection with Easter eggs is derived from the Celtic association of Hare with rebirth. It seemed that hares laid eggs, when actually "hare's nests" were those of the lapwing who builds her nest on the ground. The Christians appropriated many pagan traditions. The word "Easter" is derived from the name of the Teutonic goddess Eostra.

Hare represents the promise of spring, of rebirth, transformation, change, and new life. Hare also represents fertility and abundance, and the promise of things to come. Hare dwells on the threshold between the worlds and confers the ability to perceive signs and portents. Consequently, Hare relates to intuition and receiving messages from spirit, being attuned to the psychic realm. Hare also refers to the present and acting with speed on matters of immediate importance.

Hare reversed represents stagnation and being in a rut. There is a failure to develop or a stubborn refusal to move forward. Hare warns of procrastination, of holding back and living in the past, of clinging to irrelevant and outmoded ways. Hare reversed may warn of failure to recognize signs and portents for what they are. Most importantly, reversed Hare is a sign of pessimism and self-imposed limitation.

OTTER
Water • Fire • Earth • Air

Upright: playful, sociable, relaxed

Reversed: serious, overworked, unsociable

Direction: 226–240 degrees

Time: early August, 3–4 PM

Pace of Change: unhurried activity, as if engaged
in effortless play

OTTER · PLAYFULNESS

Otter was sacred to the Celts and appears in many Celtic myths and legends, including that of "Taliesin and Maelduin." Otter accompanied Cernunnos and was also sacred to the Irish sea god Manannan mac Lir. Cerridwen became an otter in her pursuit of Gwion. Otter is renowned for being playful. Associated with female energy, she is a delight to watch. She is graceful and acrobatic. She is friendly, curious, and sociable. She gives an air of easygoing, relaxed ease of movement. She seems to have mastered the art of self-care and found the key to happiness. She has retained the natural way of going with the flow and enjoying the moment as children do. At the same time she is protective, nurturing, and loves to share her pleasure. She has a flexible nature, is receptive to new ideas, and has a wealth of talents at her disposal. She is never happier than when playing with others and enjoying life.

Otter reversed suggests that she is not enjoying life. Perhaps it is all work and no play, no opportunity to indulge in some pleasurable activities. She may be too serious, dour, with too many responsibilities. She may be overburdened with the needs of others with no one to care about her. She needs to relax and join with others for some fun. There may be a fear of rejection, or she may be rejecting and distrustful of others. She may resent others having fun at all. She may feel terribly alone. Alternatively, she may be irresponsible and unable to take anything seriously. She may be immature and childish or needing contact with her inner child. She may be controlling and rigid, preventing others from having fun. She may be failing to protect others who need her care and attention.

HART
Water • Fire • Air • Earth

Upright: messenger, sophistication, compassion

Reversed: intolerance, harshness, lack of faith

Direction: 241–255 degrees

Time: late August, 4–5 PM

Pace of Change: steady growth, as befits developing understanding

HART · COMPASSION

In Celtic myth, the White Hart frequently appears as a messenger from the Otherworld. One such mystical Hart appeared suddenly at the marriage of Arthur and Guinevere and was pursued by Gawain. Caitlin Mathews links the White Hart with Enid's selfless love and devotion. The keyword associated with Hart is compassion. Hart is graceful, elegant, and sophisticated. She is the love of spirit, forbearing and tolerant of others. She has a healing power that derives from the One Source. She is associated with the Otherworld in a very direct way. She is the subtle messenger from the unseen realm who calls you to follow and to connect. Hart is a symbol of love. She encourages you to explore the world of spirit, to develop your own psychic abilities. She indicates the beginning of a wonderful adventure. She signals you to take note of your dreams, to be introspective, and to listen to your intuition. Hart encourages you to be open to the unusual and fey.

Hart reversed indicates harshness, lack of compassion, and intolerance. In this position she is overbearing, forceful, inconsiderate, and selfish. She lacks faith in the spiritual Otherworld and rejects all signs that come from spirit. She may be fearful of spiritual matters, seeing such things as signs of madness. Alternatively, there may be an overreliance on the spiritual realms for guidance, such that living in the mundane world becomes problematic. The physical needs of self and others may be ignored. She may need to regain a proper balance. Her love may be given lightly or only conditionally. She warns against being naive and taken for granted.

SWAN
Water • Air • Fire • Earth

Upright: transitions, art, beauty

Reversed: insensitivity, self-indulgence, ugliness

Direction: 256–270 degrees

Time: early September, 5–6 PM

Pace of Change: very gradual, as befits dawning realization

SWAN · MYSTICISM

Swan appears in several Celtic legends, most notably that of the Children of Lir. The Swan was sacred to the Celts and the Druids wore cloaks of swan feathers. In Britain, even now, swans are referred to as "the queen's birds" and it is illegal to kill one. Swan is associated with the mystical, the magical, the Otherworld. Swan indicates that spiritual matters are assuming great importance in your life and that you should pay careful attention to omens. Swan refers to astral travel and journeying in the hidden realms. Most importantly Swan indicates dawning spirituality, developing intuition, paying attention to symbolism, and having important dreams that suggest transitions and moving across the threshold between the worlds. This is often connected with artistic practices, particularly the performing arts. Swan is the flight of the soul. She refers to beauty, grace, sensitivity, and love relationships.

Swan reversed refers to a denial of the mystical or preoccupation with the Otherworld and the psychic so that you are no longer fully grounded. This can lead to neglect of self and others. You may be lost to fantasy and thus achieve little or nothing of importance in either world. Emotions may be denied or overindulged. There can be insensitivity and unfaithfulness. Artistic expression may dry up and performances may suffer. There can be a lack of aesthetic sense or you may be surrounded by ugliness.

RAVEN
Water • Earth • Air • Fire
WATER   AIR   EARTH   FIRE

Upright: prophesy, influence, synchronicity

Reversed: skepticism, unwelcome revelations, dark magic

Direction: 271–285 degrees

Time: late September, 6–7 PM

Pace of Change: very gradual, as when secrets are unraveled

RAVEN · PROPHESY

Raven is associated with Bran and the Morrighan, hence death and rebirth. Owain also had an army of ravens that fought for Arthur. The association with Bran refers to divination and oracular utterances, prophetic speech, and the revelation of the truth of a matter. The keyword associated with Raven is prophecy. Raven is also a bird connected with eloquence and with speaking different languages, thus persuasion and communication. Raven is a bird that flies straight out of the Otherworld with important messages that are often connected with change. Raven also indicates strange occurrences, synchronicity, sudden insight, and clarity. The unexpected may signal a change in consciousness leading to personal transformation. In this connection Raven confers the gift of shapeshifting. Another gift of Raven is healing energy, which often shows the influence of the ancestral realm.

Raven reversed is a sign of dark magic, harm from others, or the rebound of your own unwise actions; dabbling in things that you do not understand, forces you cannot control; blocked energy; unwelcome messages and disturbing revelations; an inability to divine with accuracy or confidence; fear of the unknown, or rejection of the Otherworld powers. This bird is the sign of the skeptic, whether yourself or another. When the Raven appears, communication suffers and there may be difficulty with self-expression. Raven reversed warns of deceit. Sometimes Raven is a sign of drastic change and a need to learn the art of shapeshifting.

SEAL
Water • Earth • Air • Fire

Upright: dreams, creativity, love

Reversed: nightmares, preoccupation, loss

Direction: 288–300 degrees

Time: early October, 7–8 PM

Pace of Change: slow and languorous, as if drifting in the ocean of the unconscious

SEAL · DREAMS

The most common reference to seals in folklore tells how they emerge from the deep and come ashore to mate with humans. In order to do this they must shed their skins and take on human form, their true origins only revealed when the hidden skin is discovered. Seal represents dreams, messages from the deep unconscious, lucid dreaming, and the call of the inner voice. This includes what have been called "big dreams," those of national or even international importance. Seal is also associated with creativity and the power of the imagination—also meditation, trance, journeying, pathworking, and other forms of altered consciousness. A powerful sense of connection with others including those departed. Seal refers to love and compassion for one's fellows, and for all forms of life, because Seal recognizes the connection that binds us all.

Seal reversed represents nightmares or a loss of connection with the inner self. The dilemma of the Seal in human form is the desire to live in both the sea and on the land. Reversed, Seal can imply confusion resulting from a lack of communication and an absence of dream messages as a result of disconnection from the unconscious realm. On another occasion the problem may be preoccupation with dreams at the expense of the mundane, resulting in self-neglect and isolation from others. There may be an inability to discriminate between fact and fiction. Reversed, Seal also warns of bewitchment. Seal often refers to loneliness and loss. This aspect of Seal may suggest lack of respect for other life forms as well as lack of compassion for other people. Sometimes she may warn of someone who does not respect the female sex, or perhaps an overbearing female.

FROG
Water • Earth • Fire • Air

Upright: healing, replenishment, metamorphosis

Reversed: pollution, resistance, insensitivity

Direction: 301–315 degrees

Time: late October, 8–9 PM

Pace of Change: slow, as if summoning refreshing rain

FROG · SENSITIVITY

Frogs are extremely sensitive to environmental changes because they inhabit both water and land, and, of course, breathe the air. It has been noted that changes in the frog population are among the very first indicators of environmental change. Thus Frog refers to sensitivity, healing, replenishment, and support. Frog can refer to personal metamorphosis or to wider change. In myth, Frog has the power to call the rains to cleanse the Earth and remove negative influences. Frog is elusive though, and often works from a hidden vantage point.

Frog reversed refers to pollution in some sense and an urgent need to clean away noxious influences. These may be emotional, physical, mental, or spiritual. There may be unfortunate change or resistance to change, either personally or more generally. The natural cycle can be disrupted. Reversed, Frog may indicate insensitivity, either emotional or environmental. There can be sickness and a need for healing.

FETCH

Keywords: the unpredictable, unaccountable, unknown

Direction: unknown

Time: unknown

Pace of Change: unknown

FETCH · CHAOS

A Fetch is an artificial spiritual entity created by wizards for specific purposes. The elemental makeup varies according to the intended purpose and consequently cannot be known without further divination. Nor can the effect of a Fetch on current work be predicted with accuracy. A Fetch may have its origin in another wizard's activities or it may be a residue of your own. You may have created the Fetch yourself for some purpose. In any event the Fetch represents the unpredictable, random features of life that can come along and alter matters unexpectedly for good or ill. The effect of the Fetch will be indicated by its position in the spread and by its orientation, whether upright or reversed. If Fetch occurs frequently, then some unknown factor is operative in your life or work. This factor can usually be attributed to someone in particular who has strong feelings toward you. Consult the oracle again for further information.

Bibliography

Anderson, R. *Celtic Oracles*. New York: Three Rivers Press, 1998.

Andrews, Ted. *How to Meet and Work with Spirit Guides*. St. Paul, MN: Llewellyn Publications, 1992.

———. *Animal-Speak: The Spiritual & Magical Powers of Creatures Great & Small*. St. Paul, MN: Llewellyn Publications, 2000.

Arroyo, S. *Astrology, Psychology, and the Four Elements: An Energy Approach to Astrology & Its Use in the Counseling Arts*. Sebastopol, CA: CRCS Publications, 1975.

Carr-Gomm, P. and S. *The Druid Animal Oracle: Working with the Sacred Animals of the Druid Tradition*. London: Connections Book Publishing Ltd., 1994.

Castaneda, Carlos. *Journey to Ixtlan: The Lessons of Don Juan*. Middlesex: Arkana, 1972.

Conway, D. J. *Animal Magick: The Art of Recognizing & Working with Familiars.* St. Paul, MN: Llewellyn Publications, 1995.

———. *Magickal Mythical Mystical Beasts: How to Invite Them into Your Life.* St. Paul, MN: Llewellyn Publications, 1996.

Guest, C. *The Mabinogian.* London: Voyager Harper-Collins, 2002.

Hope, M. *Practical Techniques of Psychic Self-Defense.* New York: St. Martin's, 1983.

Jung, C. G. *Psychology and Alchemy.* London: Routledge, 1966.

———. *Memories, Dreams, Reflections.* London: Fontana Paperbacks, 1983.

Leslie, Mike. *The Magical Personality.* St. Paul, MN: Llewellyn Publications, 2002.

Mallory, T. *Le Morte D'Arthur.* London: Studio Editions Ltd., 1990.

Mascaro, J. *The Upanishads.* Harmondsworth, Middlesex, England: Penguin Books Ltd., 1965.

Mathews, C. and J. *Ladies of the Lake.* London: Thorsons, 1992.

———. *The Western Way.* Middlesex: Arkana, 1994.

Mathews, J. *The Celtic Shaman's Pack: Exploring the Inner Worlds.* Shaftesbury, Dorset: Element Books Ltd., 1995.

Restall Orr, E. *Thorson's Principles of Druidry.* London:
Thorsons, HarperCollins, 1998.

Sams, J., and D. Carson. *Medicine Cards: The Discovery of
Power Through the Ways of Animals.* Santa Fe, NM: Bear
& Co., 1988.

Wa-Na-Nee-Che, with E. Harvey. *White Eagle Medicine
Wheel.* London: Connections Book Publishing Ltd.,
1997.

Free Magazine

Read unique articles by Llewellyn authors, recommendations by experts, and information on new releases. To receive a **free** copy of Llewellyn's consumer magazine, *New Worlds of Mind & Spirit,* simply call 1-877-NEW-WRLD or visit our website at www.llewellyn.com and click on *New Worlds.*

LLEWELLYN ORDERING INFORMATION

Order Online:
Visit our website at www.llewellyn.com, select your books, and order them on our secure server.

Order by Phone:
- Call toll-free within the U.S. at 1-877-NEW-WRLD (1-877-639-9753). Call toll-free within Canada at 1-866-NEW-WRLD (1-866-639-9753)
- We accept VISA, MasterCard, and American Express

Order by Mail:
Send the full price of your order (MN residents add 7% sales tax) in U.S. funds, plus postage & handling to:
Llewellyn Worldwide
P.O. Box 64383, Dept. 0-7387-0505-5
St. Paul, MN 55164-0383, U.S.A.

Postage & Handling:

Standard (U.S., Mexico, & Canada). If your order is:
$49.99 and under, add $3.00
$50.00 and over, FREE STANDARD SHIPPING

AK, HI, PR: $15.00 for one book plus $1.00 for each additional book.

International Orders (airmail only):
$16.00 for one book plus $3.00 for each additional book

Shapeshifter Tarot
Illustrated by Lisa Hunt

D. J. CONWAY
AND SIRONA KNIGHT

Like the ancient Celts, you can now practice the shamanic art of shapeshifting and access the knowledge of the eagle, the oak tree, or the ocean: wisdom that is inherently yours and resides within your very being. *The Shapeshifter Tarot* kit is your bridge between humans, animals, and nature. The cards in this deck act as merging tools, allowing you to tap into many different animal energies together with the elemental qualities of air, fire, water, and earth.

The accompanying book gives detailed explanations on how to use the cards, along with their full esoteric meanings, and mythological and magical roots. Exercises in shapeshifting and doubling out, moving through gateways, meditation, and guided imagery give you the opportunity to enhance your levels of perception and awareness, allowing you to hone and accentuate your magical understanding and skill.

1-56718-384-0 $29.95
Boxed kit includes 81 full-color cards, and instruction book

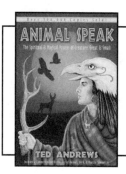

Animal-Speak
The Spiritual & Magical Powers of Creatures Great & Small

TED ANDREWS

The animal world has much to teach us. Some animals are experts at survival and adaptation, some never get cancer, and some embody strength and courage, while others exude playfulness. Animals remind us of the potential we can unfold, but before we can learn from them, we must first be able to speak with them.

In this book, myth and fact are combined in a manner that will teach you how to speak and understand the language of the animals in your life. *Animal-Speak* helps you meet and work with animals as totems and spirits—by learning the language of their behaviors within the physical world. It provides techniques for reading signs and omens in nature so you can open yourself to higher perceptions and even prophecy. It reveals the hidden, mythical, and realistic roles of 45 animals, 60 birds, 8 insects, and 6 reptiles.

Animals will become a part of you, revealing to you the majesty and divine in all life. They will restore your childlike wonder of the world and strengthen your belief in magic, dreams, and possibilities.

0-87542-028-1, 400 pp., 7 x 10, illus., photos   **$19.95**

TO WRITE TO THE AUTHOR

If you wish to contact the author or would like more information about this book, please write to the author in care of Llewellyn Worldwide and we will forward your request. Both the author and publisher appreciate hearing from you and learning of your enjoyment of this book and how it has helped you. Llewellyn Worldwide cannot guarantee that every letter written to the author can be answered, but all will be forwarded. Please write to:

Mike Leslie
℅ Llewellyn Worldwide
P.O. Box 64383, Dept. 0-7387-0505-5
St. Paul, MN 55164-0383, U.S.A.

Please enclose a self-addressed stamped envelope for reply, or $1.00 to cover costs. If outside U.S.A., enclose international postal reply coupon.

Many of Llewellyn's authors have websites with additional information and resources. For more information, please visit our website at http://www.llewellyn.com